SMALL
SPACE
LIVING

Christine Brun

4880 Lower Valley Road Atglen, Pennsylvania 19310

Dedication

To my mother and father, who taught me the importance of home.

Other Schiffer Books on Related Subjects

Design Chronicles: Significant Mass-Produced Designs of the 20th Century. Carroll Gantz. ISBN: 0764322230. $79.95

Furniture by Harrods. Harrods Ltd. of London. ISBN: 0887401805. $24.95

Mexican style, sustainable. Tina Skinner. ISBN: 9780764327438. $19.95

Nomadic Furniture. D-I-Y Projects that are Lightweight & Light on the Environment. James Hennessey & Victor Papanek. ISBN: 9780764330247. $29.99

Rattan Furniture: Tropical Comfort Throughout The House. Harvey Schwartz. ISBN: 0764307703. $39.95

Small Italian Villas & Farmhouses. Guy Lowell. ISBN: 9780764327063. $39.95

Traditional Mexican Style Interiors. Donna McMenamin. ISBN: 0764316931. $39.95

Copyright © 2009 by Christine Brun
Library of Congress Control Number: 2008938356

Cover and book designed by: Bruce Waters
Type set in Bernhard Modern BT/Humanist 521 BT

ISBN: 978-0-7643-3192-3
Printed in China

Contents

Acknowledgments

This book would have never come to be without the wisdom of my friend and former editor at Copley News Service, Glenda Winders. In the fall of 1997, I was asked to audition for the column *Small Spaces*, along with a few other designer/writers. When I was awarded the job, Glenda said to me, "Right now you are a designer who happens to write. When I get finished with you, you will be a writer who also happens to be a designer!" She made me look good and believed in me year after year. Thank you, Glenda. She and her former boss, Bob Witty, conceived of the column and an observant national sales staff at Copley felt that there was a niche for a column focused on small living spaces. I am grateful for their insight into the future of housing.

I wish to thank Rosalie Domingues for her help with prying photographs out of people and following up with phone calls. Not enough can be said about one Catie Carroll Henoch of Carthage, Illinois – my incredibly energetic and dedicated assistant. We are designers during the day and it was a huge challenge to sandwich writing, editing, scanning, and emailing into our regular work day with our own clients. Without Catie, this book would not have been finished. I owe her a debt of gratitude for her computer skills and patience with my computer challenged middleaged mind.

Special thanks to The Hardwood Information Center, who shared their members' images with us. Christina McDonald at DRS & Associates was extremely helpful and did an outstanding job. The people at FLOR and The Container Store were wonderful in sharing their images with us. Amanda Cortese at Meredith was terrific in getting us images from Country Home. I thank Barbara Metz for her advice about publicizing this book and an older thank you for putting me in touch originally with Glenda Winders at Copley about the opportunity to write my column.

And then there is my adorable husband who has always believed in my writing. When I first got the column assignment, he had a trophy made for me that says "Designer-Writer Extraordinaire". He has always been proud of me and nurturing in a loving way. Trying to be helpful, he brought me a newspaper article from Mexico City that told how the city was running out of cemetery space! Apparently city officials began a campaign to encourage families to consider cremation instead of traditional underground burial. My sweetheart saw this as a small space story in the extreme sense and thought it would help me out. He's inimitable and I thank him for his love and constant support.

Introduction
Small Spaces

Those who grew up in a classic three bedroom 1950s house might not accurately remember it as a small place. In reality, those homes were only an average size of around 983 square feet. The children of that generation aspired to larger and better homes as part of the post WWII prosperity, so that by 2004 the average home in the United States was around 2,350 square feet. Inevitably every trend eventually corrects by shifting and over the last few years a steady reversal has begun as new floor plans slim down in a less-is-more movement.

This particular three bedroom plan had only one full bathroom, with a half-bath in the master. In some parts of the country space was greatly expanded by completing a full basement. *Courtesy of Homemaster Publications, Jamaica, New York.*

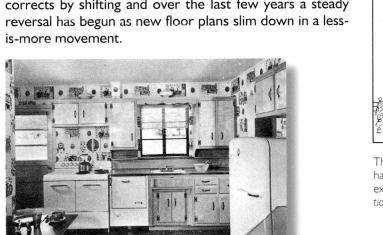

As a part of a 1,315 square foot home, this 13 foot by 13 foot kitchen featured "in-kitchen" dining that was visible from the front foyer. *Courtesy of Homemaster Publications, Jamaica, New York.*

Ranch style homes were wildly popular in the 1950s and emphasized family living. This was a modest 1,116 square foot home designed in 1957 by Architect Rudolph A. Matern. *Courtesy of Homemaster Publications, Jamaica, New York.*

This new inclination is due in part to changing demographics, and is partly owed to higher costs of land and construction. As the housing market woes deepen, inflation affects the overall economy, and utility costs continue to escalate, we can now say definitively that the size of the typical U.S. home is declining. Philosophical changes about what we can expect from our homes have also been noted. Uncertain economic times keep people in their smaller homes and thinking of ways to improve the function and aesthetics of what they already own.

"The recent weakness in the housing market forces households to be more sensitive to housing affordability concerns. Coupled with rising home energy costs, this encourages many to rethink their overall space needs," says American Institute of Architects (AIA) Chief Economist Kermit Baker, PhD, Hon. AIA. Home improvement has become nearly a national pastime thanks to television programs that examine home interiors from the sublime to the wretched. Even in a sluggish market homeowners look for ways to spiff up and create a selling point by remodeling a kitchen or bath.

For the last nine years I have written a weekly column called *Small Spaces* for Copley News Service that focuses on living spaces of 1,200 square feet or less. Having nearly 6 million readers, I have learned first hand of the frustrations experienced by people as they try to locate appropriately sized furnishings, appliances, and fixtures for small space living. It seems that it's not really the size of a home that might be upsetting people, but not being able to easily access information regarding products made for the small home that grinds.

Europe and Japan are far ahead of the United States when it comes to making the most of small living spaces because these populations have lived in cramped homes for generations. They don't seem to whine about it like we Americans often do, because they accept the architectural limitations as a part of life in ancient cities or towns by embracing outstanding design. We as a society have much to learn from their experiences and product development ideas.

Country home with screened porch adds to usable living space. *Courtesy of Mosquito Curtains.*

Town homes, the modern row house, often offer garages. There is generally no yard, only small balconies or patios. *Courtesy of Rich Legg.*

The famous Painted Ladies in San Francisco are Victorian era small homes and, despite their age and limited space, still are quite expensive. *Courtesy of Art Kowalsky.*

Scandinavians also have adapted and invented furniture and products expertly. The best hardware – the ingredient that enables things to slide, telescope out, flip up, or hang off walls – comes from Germany, Sweden, or Japan. Smaller sized appliances are made for the Asian and European markets that offer superior function and flexibility. Haier® is a Chinese owned company that is one of the world's leading home appliance manufacturers that has introduced a convertible bottom drawer refrigerator. With a drawer that converts from a refrigerator to a freezer and back again, consumers can change one space to meet storage needs at the time. Small space demands flexibility from furnishings and other more utilitarian devices such as plumbing fixtures and appliances.

The Aga *Companian* cooker is 24" wide, and originally designed to be used with their larger ranges. *Courtesy of Aga Heartland.*

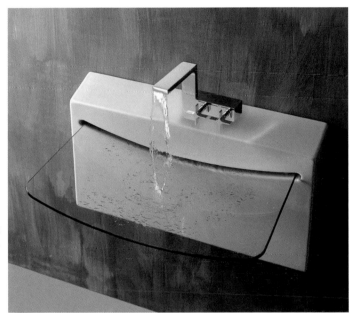

Lacava Block Crystal Wash Basin is a typical Euro-style basin that hangs off the wall and visually opens up a small bathroom. *Courtesy of Lacava.*

Europeans consider kitchen cabinets and equipment as furniture and take them from home to home when they move. *Triple Modular Unit with Space for Sink* by the French company Grange. *Courtesy of Grange.*

My goal is to bring to the U.S. homeowner of 1,220 square feet or less the same valuable information already known by much of the world and maybe to encourage U.S. manufacturers to pay more attention to this burgeoning market. As some predictions indicate, the boomers will flock towards cities in record numbers after abandoning complicated suburban lifestyles, no longer necessary after raising their families or coming to the end of a working career. The urbanization of baby boomers promises to put pressure on the design industry in new ways as boomers stipulate convenience and luxury. We will begin to see a new kind of shrinking home, defined by expanded demands for not only function, but also style and glamour.

The luxurious Humidrawer™ fits into a standard wine cellar 23.875" wide x 24.25" deep x 34" high. *Courtesy of Marvel Industries.*

Bora tub by Neptune is a corner tub with a diamond shape that is perfect to give an enlarged perception of a small bathroom. *Courtesy of Neptune.*

For instance, we are looking at a population that has come to love the serenity and drama of the spa experience. In order to deliver smaller soaking tubs set on warm floors, Americans may need to access foreign merchandise or copy their designs for tiny tubs. Glamorous fixtures can be hung off the walls to save space. Europeans long have preferred to use vertical space. They hang toilets, sinks, cabinets, and thereby eliminate clumsy swinging cabinet doors that require clearances. Our European cousins opt for covers that glide up and down or side to side in space-saving ease!

Over the years as I penned my column it occurred to me that someone should gather all of the resource information into one place that would aid in more sophisticated design solutions for the smaller home. Editors are not fond of promoting one manufacturer over another and so very rarely were any of the manufacturers or model numbers identified for my readers, much to my own frustration. After hearing from scores of aggravated readers time after time, eventually it occurred to me that *I* ought to write my own book and solve part of the challenge regarding sourcing solutions for the small house.

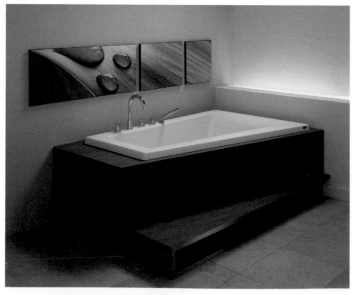

The *Bora* is part of the Zen Line and is 32" wide at the narrow end and 60" long. *Courtesy of Neptune.*

As you may have already discovered, when planning and designing limited space, there is no room for error. There is a pressing need for unique solutions to problems. When you cannot waste an inch of space there is definitely more at risk. My columns have offered advice about how designers, architects, and homeowners resolve problems in small spaces.

It is my hope and intention that this book becomes a useful and practical resource for people trying to make small homes into their dream places. Everyone wants a good place to live that works for them. Those working with tight space limitations encounter a few more challenges in making home a comfortable, stylish, and magical place to live.

Tiny cottages designed by architect Mary Ann Cusato, originally for victims of Hurricane Katrina, range between 544 square feet and 936 square feet. Compact built-ins make the cottage extremely functional. *Courtesy of Cusato Cottages.*

Much smaller sized upholstered pieces and dining furniture necessary when you live in just three rooms. *Courtesy of Maine Cottage.*

Chapter One
Why Small Spaces?

A small home can be celebrated as deliciously cozy or it can become an irritating place that you apologize for when it does not function well. We find that people choose small homes for an assortment of reasons from a love of the intimate style to being financially limited to an older neighborhood with more modestly sized houses. Almost everyone who lives in a cramped place struggles with wanting it to look larger and to work harder for them.

The Cusato Cottage was designed in a way that homeowners can add to the basic footprint over time, growing a 500 square foot unit into a home over 1,000 square feet.
Courtesy Lowe's Home Improvement.

Tiny cottage kits offer an affordable way to build a guest room on your property or a tiny get-away home at a separate location. *Courtesy of Jamaica Cottage.*

From seniors looking to down-size, to 30-somethings buying their first home, to folks figuring out a small guest house on a larger property, we find that planning for limited space is very dependent upon locating the right ingredients. Apartments fill a need for more than 50 million Americans living in more than 33 million spaces. The average size of a U.S. apartment has been 900 square feet for more than 20 years now. Renters are even more limited in the type of things that they can do to make their tiny homes run well.

An apartment of 700 to 900 square feet often means that several different functions are open to one another. *Courtesy Room & Board.*

It is true that the movement towards smaller homes has been on the rise, even before the present housing crisis, since the 1970s for two reasons: One is high housing costs and the other is a shift to smaller families and changing lifestyles. In the last few years another reason is the advent of senior citizenship for millions of baby boomers who are rumored to be attracted to moving back into the city for a myriad of social reasons. These same boomers are fond of smallish vacation homes, and a good number have the resources to own a get-away place that most often tends to be smaller than a main residence.

Proper storage is critical for the garage too, if you want to coax more function from the interior spaces when they are free from clutter. Platinum elfa® Garage Gardening Center *Courtesy of The Container Store®.*

Organization is more important in a small home. elfa® Platinum Mesh Drawers provide storage for items kids need easy access to and allow a family room to work extra hard for the homeowner. *Courtesy of The Container Store®.*

Hardly a new idea, but suddenly little houses are being regarded refreshingly in a more positive way. Some people just honestly prefer small space living even when they might afford a much larger home because they like the efficiency and intimacy delivered by a cottage. A bigger pile of stuff does not necessarily make one's life better in any way. The famous quote by Mies van der Rohe proclaimed that "less is more" is embraced by those who participate in the voluntary simplicity movement.

In Cecile Andrews' book, *The Circle of Simplicity,* she outlines how and why people seek a simple lifestyle. Mostly, she stresses getting in touch with your own wisdom and truths as the world around you becomes more complex with time. Life in the past did offer less stress in some ways. In 1903 for instance, only 14% of the homes in our country had a bathtub and fewer had a telephone. At that time there were only 8,000 cars in the entire nation and because of fewer automobiles, there were fewer paved roads. The lust for speed had not yet overcome Americans; the maximum speed limit in most cities was 10 miles per hour, so naturally life was much less stressful. Not to mention there were no cell phones, computers, and I-Phones to add even more pressure to the average lifestyle.

The 1,500 square foot, one-room weekend retreat designed by Ludwig Mies Van Der Rohe might be considered the grandfather to weekend retreats and home offices sold as pre-fabricated kits.

With progress and the easy availability of goods and improvements, came an immensely more complex lifestyle. Henry David Thoreau said, "Most of the luxuries, and many of the so-called comforts of life, are not only not indispensable, but positive hindrances to the elevation of mankind. With respect to luxuries and comforts, the wisest have never lived a more simple and meager life than the poor." A simple life means a kind of freedom from following the agenda that someone else sets out for you and it is a kind of emancipation from clutter and conspicuous consumption. Some of the hidden benefits to a small home are reduced costs of heating and cooling, lower energy consumption, lower furnishing costs, and less maintenance. But many of us have to evolve over a long time to come to a place where we can be happy living with less.

There are those who can be defined in psychological terms as highly sensitive types and they often find a small place easier to handle emotionally. It fits them better because there is essentially much less to worry about regarding the maintenance of a tiny home. These are gentle souls who often find normal daily tasks to be daunting and who shy away from complicated living situations. My own husband was one of these people when I found him – a bachelor at fifty-three. His most pleasant memory was of an apartment he had when he was in law school. "It was so small," he would coo when describing it to me, "that I just rolled out of bed and into my desk chair!" You will never convince him that this wasn't the most perfect place he ever lived! While those ship-like quarters would have made me crazy, he took real comfort in how manageable a situation it was for him.

Beautiful articles do not take up a lot of space and fresh flowers do wonders for any room. *Courtesy of About-Flowers.com.*

Regardless of size, one of the most ancient predispositions of man is the desire for a permanent and personal home. Small or large, fancy or simple, we humans all yearn for a place to call home that has a special meaning and is filled with the things we love. I recall consulting with a woman who was refreshing the larger house in a posh neighborhood where she raised her family and now kept as a rental property. She and her husband however preferred an 800 square foot beach cottage for their own home. Cheerfully I was told how much she prized living in her diminutive cottage. "My husband and I see much more of each other, the garden is small and easy to care for, and we adore the lifestyle at the beach!" she gushed with a joy that was genuine. This couple own a lot of rental properties that are larger than their beach cottage, but happily prefer life in one of their smallest homes.

It cost Thoreau $28.12 to build his cabin retreat. You can buy it fully assembled for your own yard for $22,500 or buy a kit with building guide for $14,500. *Courtesy Thoreau Society.*

As new housing costs increase rapidly in rejuvenated urban settings and in many suburban locales, many people show interest in staying put and remodeling to meet changing family needs and wants. Particularly in the wake of 9/11 there is a definite shift in social patterns, as people tend to stay home more. Some have dubbed it "cocooning" as there is an increased interest in making our homes more comfortable and a respite from the outer world. According to the National Association of Home Builders, over 26 million Americans spend more than $180 billion on home improvements each year as home turns into sanctuary.

This whimsical built-in desk area might serve as a home office or homework area. *Courtesy of Smith + Noble.*

Remodeling for the small home owner presents particular challenges that I hope this book can alleviate. For instance: A new baby is coming and the one bedroom of a sweet bungalow must stretch to make more room. Who makes baby furniture that might have to live in the dining room and look good with the other furniture? Is there a way to close off the dining room when the baby is napping? Could the baby sleep in an alcove created by removing a closet? A newly unemployed business professional is obligated to convert one of two bedrooms into functional and presentable workspace in order to join the ranks of millions of Americans who work from home. Can that office furniture share space with the guest room? How can the mess be closed off at a moment's notice? In addition to locating appropriate furniture for the purpose, maybe more radical solutions are in order. Such changes may mean adding a room over the garage or constructing a 100 square foot out-building on your property in order to provide function.

We see yet another population—the oldest boomers—are tending to stay in their homes and remodel instead of moving to a retirement facility. The habitat industry, including builders, architects, and interior designers, are now calling this approach *aging in place*. Boomers want their homes designed so that they can gracefully age in familiar surroundings with both independence and dignity. At the same time, they represent the largest home buying population in the United States and the housing industry is watching this demographic carefully. The National Association of Home Builders (NAHB) offers a unique certification for building and design professionals so that they might provide consumers with comprehensive and practical aging-in-place solutions as they spend money to retrofit existing home and plan new homes for seniors. There are relatively small improvements to an existing home, like adding a ramp to the front door and improving exterior lighting that can make life easier. More invasive solutions might be to add an elevator for access to a second floor, or design a no-step shower entry.

Another twist on this idea is making a place for aging parents who come to live with their adult children. Space must be either modified to be safe and appropriate, or new space must be added. Remodeling in both of these circumstances can be even more stressful than ordinary building projects. If it is the home of the failing parent that is being reworked, it is generally useful to have an adult child involved to help facilitate decision making, paper work, and contact with the builder. While a parent may resist hands-on involvement by an adult child, it is advisable to provide some sort of oversight. It is important to assemble a team of capable and trustworthy professionals who will not take advantage of an elderly parent. No matter how you arrange to work, it is vital that the design team know who the real decision maker is and how to get critical judgments made in an expeditious manner.

A typical granny flat often combines living and sleeping functions into one room and dividing up the space with a TV wall is a good solution. Flat screen TV here saves valuable space. *Courtesy of Philips Electronics.*

Chapter Two
Who Lives In Small Spaces Anyway?

Very long ago, during the Old Stone Age, man lived in caves or in the found shelter under stone outcroppings in lush river valleys. People were gatherers and hunters who moved with the seasons and animal herds. The concept of a permanent, less vulnerable home was not known until humans learned to feed themselves more proficiently and experienced the luxury of settling in one place for longer periods of time. Once that happened villages began and were made up of deliberately built, not found, dwellings. Individual lodgings were planted in a safe place and were made from wood, mud, and grasses. These organic materials decompose readily and so there is actually little left to study from early times, with few exceptions.

Evidence of furniture, as well as houses, built of wood and mud from 6,000 years ago in what is now modern Turkey, has been discovered and studied. While the ancient Egyptians, Babylonians, Persians, Greeks, and Romans all developed more refined and unique building methods over time, often what we have left of these civilizations are palaces, monolithic ceremonial or burial structures, and tombs rather than individual family homes. Rare glimpses into everyday life in a bustling Roman port town are offered by the unique remnants in cities like Pompeii or Herculaneum. But in general, we have little left of ancient homes to study first hand.

Many of the American Indian tribes made portable tee pees from hides that were perfect as the tribe traveled seasonally. This is available for purchase. *Photographer: Glenn Swanson courtesy of www.tipi.com.*

Western Europeans may have originally reached our shores before peoples from Asia by actually crossing the Atlantic in simple vessels. Tools discovered on the American plain are similar to those found near the site of Cro-Magnon man in southwestern France and in other Western European sites, leading some scientists to believe that North America was visited by early European tribes before any migration of people down from the frozen Alaskan trail. This fuels the argument that even Scandinavians might have made it across the Atlantic in long boats. Originally North America had native dwelling types that included: *teepees, kivas, chickees, wigwams, igloos, long houses, and multi-family cliff houses* of interconnecting rooms.

Once white Europeans reached our shores, people lived differently in deliberately constructed little structures made of wood. You have only to visit Williamsburg, Virginia, Boston, Massachusetts, or Old Town in Newport, Rhode Island, to see for yourself how small the first pubs, shops, and private homes were at the very beginning of colonization in America. There is a literal historic trail from the original cottages of England to those in the colonies. Few of those structures built before the 17th century survived intact, but remnants indicate that these early cottages were a single room built from sticks and mud, with low ceilings.

Rounded thatched pallozas of Celtic origin in Spain show primitive shelter structures made from found materials. *Photographer: Robert Harding Picture Library Ltd.*

The word *pueblo* means "stone masonry village dweller" in Spanish. Complexes similar to the modern apartment building were built with interconnecting rooms and homes. This multi-storied pueblo is in Taos, New Mexico. *Photographer: Chuck Place.*

These cottages were actually grim, windowless places and smoke from the fire was simply allowed to escape through an open door. Cottages were simple configurations, just a minuscule level better than huts that took only a few days for eager colonists to put together with available materials. People cooked and mainly worked outdoors, and merely slept in the basic shelters. So it was that cottages were built by the colonists according to the particular traditions brought with them to the new land. When the Europeans arrived in America, the most obvious influence over the style of building was the country of origin for the owner or craftsman involved in the construction. Since the building materials were whatever was available in the local area, they ranged from stone, unbaked earth-turf, cob (clay, chalk, and small stones), bricks, timbers, branches, reeds, thatch, clay tiles, stone, and slates.

The young country began to witness uniquely American interpretations of the architectural styles of England, France, and Spain, built with available native materials that added unique nuances to the old world styles. Initially crude and simple structures were all that was needed as basic shelter from the wilderness. Well-known Yankee pragmatism over-ruled fashion when builders were trying to make time against the threat of inhospitable weather. In early colonial times, all rooms were multi-purpose out of necessity and you could expect to see a bed in every room. Fireplace, dining surface, food preparation area, and storage were arranged in one open room.

A section of wall construction at the Jamestown settlement in Virginia shows a combination of locally available building materials. *Photographer Christine Brun.*

An early American cabin in Maryland.
Photographer: Archade.

It makes me smile to recognize that people today might face the same design and space challenges in studios, mobile homes, or a one bedroom urban condo that colonists endured in their one room cabin! Save the modern exceptions like electronics, media equipment, and appliances, Americans today could find themselves living in one big open room that has to function like those colonial cabins. Instead of a barn, most city dwellers need a place to keep the modern horse with four tires. People who live and work in the heart of a major city often try to do completely without a car of their own. They take public transportation, rent a flex-car when needed, or hire a driver.

A renovated 600 square foot condo in Seattle with built-ins made of sustainable apple plywood and maple veneer. Plastic laminate is added for color and a ladder gets the user to the higher storage spots. *Design by Kerf Design. Courtesy of Nathan Hartman.*

When we consider contemporary Americans who live in small houses we learn what their choice in housing says about them as individuals. As an interior designer, I have often heard near apologies from people who live in limited space such as, *"Well, I just have a small house,"* or *"It's just a condo, but I really do like nice things."* I've often wondered to myself where the negative connotations about living in a small house come from anyway? Why do some people feel like they must explain their small house circumstances? I believe that my own prejudice came innocently enough from my mother, who imprinted me with the idea that a small house was just not as good as a big one!

I remember her saying that someone we knew " lived in a place smaller than a broom closet!" It seems like I heard that little ditty more than once while growing up. My mother and father were part of the generation that experienced a severe housing shortage in our country, post-World War II. My parents lived in Los Angeles and the only reason that they even had a place to live was that my grandmother owned a little rental duplex. In fact, they shared the single bathroom with another tenant. I remember hearing what sounded to a little girl like nightmarish stories about how they had to share a bathroom with this stranger – a nurse – who was extremely sloppy! In my house, being dirty was next to a mortal sin and always inexcusable. The net result was the story about living in this little place sounded negative to me.

A slick apartment in Miami Beach, Florida, combines multiple functions in one-room living. *Courtesy of Trend USA.*

Then there were my own memories of the new house my family moved into when we came to San Diego, California, from Costa Mesa when I was around five and a half years old. In the way that houses of our childhood get distorted in memory, it seemed like an immense place to me. Our little family consisted of three little girls under the age of eight, a baby on the way, and our young parents. The house was built on a mesa atop one of the thousands of canyons that define the landscape of the city and the actual development pushed against the northern edges of the city at that time. It was a typical 1957 ranch-style floor plan of three bedrooms, 2 bathrooms, living room, dining room with a breakfast bar, and the kitchen. We welcomed my little brother to that house and lived there until I was approaching seventh grade. My parents kept the house as a rental after our family moved in order to be within walking distance to the Catholic school that we all attended. Because they held onto that property, I was able to move back in to that house as a young married woman in 1976. Not all people get the chance to revisit a childhood home as an adult, let alone experience living there again. It was an interesting experience and I got to see for myself that the place was not at all how it loomed in my child mind.

Small bungalows became popular in the 1920s and 1930s in Spanish Revival style and Craftsman style. *Photographer: Michael Beiriger.*

Digging deeper and beyond my personal experience growing up, I believe that the descriptive assignment of "inadequate" to a small and unpretentious home could be based on primitive thinking about strength, dominance, and leadership. It's the idea that the better hunter has more meat to comfortably feed and clothe his family unit. A modern guy who makes a lot of money can afford to buy his wife a huge diamond ring, a $60,000 car, and an expensive sprawling house. It's a symbol of a kind of superiority based solely on materialism. It is therefore assumed that if you rent, it is because you cannot afford to own your own home and therefore this situation is supposed to be a kind of failing. And, like it or not, this is the land of highly valued independence, nowhere more clearly visible than in the hard-held American belief in home ownership as an ultimate achievement. Own or rent, people living in small houses very often feel that they have to explain it to others and that seems to be unfortunate.

I believe that we can change the unconscious response that bigger is better, as it relates to our homes, if we analyze where it originates in our collective and personal history. Over time as I've researched topics for my weekly column, I have taught myself to have a different attitude toward the small house. Now I actually feel dedicated to bolstering the popularity of the small house because I've learned how satisfying cottages can become when well planned. In every part of the country, some of the most fashionable and costly real estate might actually translate into extremely small houses with skimpy yards, no yard at all, or just a balcony! There are many good things to be said for the reputation of the smaller home.

An aerial view of Levittown, New York. In 1947, potato fields were developed into the first mass-produced suburban tract based on extreme economy and the idea that the little houses could eventually be expanded upward and outward. They sold originally for under $8,000. *Courtesy of Levittown History Collection*

The Cape Cod style homes were joined in 1949 by the Ranch style houses that eliminated basements, poured cement slabs, and put the plumbing right into the slab. The 1950 ranch homes came with a carport and a 12.5" Admiral TV. *Courtesy of Levittown History Collection.*

Row houses in Chelsea, London. *Photographer: VI*

An old neighborhood oozing with architectural charm can often trump newer areas with much larger cookie-cutter houses. That is because neighborhoods packed with enchanting smaller homes pulse with visual delights that are uniquely varied from house to house. Often gorgeous old growth trees arch over streets. Low walls made from bricks or cement and wrought iron work identify yards in haphazard fashion, as do picket fences. Architectural styles from generations past ply our curiosity in neighborhoods where each home is unique and quirky.

With all these warm, fuzzy feelings floating around, why then is there still some downbeat sense about the little home? My theory is rooted in history as far back as the dark ages of Western Europe, when the dirt poor lived in insignificant, shabby places and the great lord lived in a castle or large hall. Both of these straightforward shelter types were equally dark, damp, and bereft of much comfort. A king or a serf essentially survived in the same rudimentary way without the convenience of indoor plumbing or indoor bathrooms, sans central heating or electricity. The lord of the castle might have been able order glass as one exotic luxury of the middle ages, but nonetheless he too dined by dim and smoky torch light just like the poor. Horses ambled into his great hall from a breezy courtyard entrance and they shared the muddy straw-covered stone floor with men and other animals. It must have been smelly and filthy exactly like the peasant's homestead shared with sheep, chickens, and donkeys. Therefore it was only the comparative *size* of the home that distinguished an individual's status in life from any other man's. While we have found many other ways to distinguish success, somehow throughout history, the idea that the bigger house is superior still stubbornly lingers on.

I believe that it is possible that those who live in small homes still feel some residue of the disadvantaged from hundreds and hundreds of years ago. The measure of achievement in our country is often tied to the size of one's home, rather than education or personal accomplishments. With this attitude in place we might be inclined to blindly miss the best part about small houses. There is some evidence that even little kids seem to make determinations about people based on the size of the house that they own. When my mom said, "...smaller than a broom closet," I thought that she was talking about a pretty bad thing.

In a BBC film sequence, the development of 25 five year olds was followed from birth. The series, *Child of Our Time*, studied how the kids' views of the world have already been shaped by the stereotypes held by adults and how the children themselves fit into the world. An interesting exercise had the kids playing with two very different looking dolls' houses. One was painted to look like gray stone, with stucco, pillars, and something like five bedrooms. The other was made to look like a narrow, red brick terrace house.

Once the children had played with the houses they were asked some questions about the kind of people who might live in these houses. Interestingly enough, these young children were quick to say that rich people live in big houses; the poor live in small ones! Many added swiftly that a child living in a big house is a happy child. When asked about the life of the poor child, we learn that her parents "...aren't very nice to her and they hit her." Other exercises indicated that the little kids thought that *good people* lived in large houses and bad people lived in the small places. Tessa Livingstone, the executive producer of the series, and a psychologist who has studied children extensively, explained the origins of such views: "They come from a combination of society's expectations that permeate through the language of the way we speak on television and in our homes, and the teachers and nurseries, and through games and toys, and through the direct experience they have of life in the particular circumstances." Could our adult reaction to diminutive houses shift to the negative because of childhood impressions? Could the pangs and challenges that most people feel when facing downsizing be rooted in much deeper angst? Understanding all of this might encourage a little more respect for ourselves and others who are trying to get homes to function at the highest level despite size.

A guest bedroom can double as a library in a two bedroom home. This storage ottoman opens into a single bed with headboard. *Photographer: Kelly Ishikawa courtesy of Gump's.*

There are many legitimate reasons that people choose smaller homes besides not being able to afford bigger real estate. Some folks choose to scale down as they become empty nesters and look for more freedom from sizable property and the maintenance drudgery that goes along with it. Many Americans, fed up with the rat race, decide that they wish to live more simply and not be a slave to a large mortgage, high utility bills and upkeep costs. Some find themselves in fleeting situations that require them to be somewhere for a short period of time: A temporary job assignment, being assigned to university housing, newly graduated children returning home, or adult children moving home to care for an aging parent. Other people suddenly face living in a tiny place if they are temporarily separated people, newly divorced couples, and recently retired couples looking for a new community in which to live.

A fireplace and two chairs are enough to make a comfortable setting. *Courtesy of Heat and Glo*

Loft living appeals to some and sliding doors offer a creative way to divide the space. *Courtesy of The Sliding Door Co., San Diego, CA.*

Empty nesters might abandon formal dining in favor of a more relaxed and space conscious setting right in the kitchen itself. *Courtesy of Roomscapes Design Center.*

Finally, some people simply *feel* better, more cozy and contented, in more manageable room sizes. One of my clients purchased a tiny historic Spanish Revival style home built in 1929 located just blocks from the Pacific Ocean. This couple raised their family in a larger home out in the suburbs, but now wanted to change their lifestyle. He and his wife wanted to improve their health by walking on the beach, which was now only two blocks away, and they wanted to down-size. I think that he said it best when he filled out our usual client questionnaire: "Love grows best in small places." When I say those words out loud I realize how lovely it is to be happy with just enough, rather than always craving more and more stuff.

Style does not have to be sacrificed for size: This 48" claw foot tub fits into the smallest bathroom. *Courtesy of Country Home.*

Empty Nesters

The much talked about *empty nester* category is generally thought of in terms of a couple or single person in middle age, in good health, and with an assumed amount of financial comfort. We often find that folks in this group have sold or are thinking of selling their larger family quarters and want to seriously simplify their lifestyle. This invariably involves setting up house in a much smaller place. Generally this kind of change gives them a lifestyle independent of children, and instead of spending time cleaning, maintaining, and repairing living area, tending to a yard and garage, they carve out free time for various recreational pursuits.

Empty nesters look forward to no more kids' activities on the weekends and replace sitting at the soccer field with bike riding, golf, or tennis. Even less active people with grown children or no children want to spend time pursuing likes and hobbies, reading, traveling, and just plain taking it easier! Often a move to a smaller home, but in a more expensive area, is possible because they can now afford the more desirable spot and can get along with the smaller space.

The road to liberty starts with a tiny bit of angst because one must decide what possessions to keep and which must be pitched or given away. There is often a rather painful and nostalgic sifting through years' worth of belongings and treasures. This is the most negative part of scaling back for nearly everyone regardless of age. Everyone, except oddly enough my own dear mother who apparently loves to throw things out: She once handed my lovely yellow prom dress that she had made by hand to a street person walking in the alley behind her home in a burst of purging. Seriously, it can be difficult to part with treasured items accumulated over a lifetime.

There are several classic examples of empty nesters from my own clientele list, each with a different story: My first example was the Director of Planning for a large city who was a 60 year old widow with two grown sons. She was vibrantly immersed in her career and wanted to move into the heart of the city for which she worked from the suburbs. She was ready to give up a classic 3-bedroom house with a good-sized front and back yard. After selling her 2,500 square foot home she moved within walking distance of her city hall office into a 1,200 square foot condo. There were only two bedrooms and a very tiny balcony with barely enough room for a little round patio table and a few potted plants. However, she had a sparkling view of downtown lights at night, a peek-a-boo look at the water, and bustling city scenes to enjoy.

We busied ourselves removing one wall between the living room and dinning room, thereby creating one large living room where two smaller rooms had been. Her move into the city allowed her to work long hours and still engage in after work exercise and a social life. Not only did she give intimate dinner parties for friends and colleagues, this high level manager invited her entire department – some 70 people – and easily managed by freely placing food in every room of her home. She was successful at entertaining because she was willing to abandon rigid ideas about guests that may have applied well in her former home. Instead this positive woman adapted breezily to what space was now available and never missed a beat.

My next example was an athletic middle-aged couple with five grandchildren who sold their mobile home finance business and used that milestone to also sell their large suburban home with considerable acreage. They raised their family in that country home with horses and plenty of quiet, yet they now wanted to experience a full urban life. For a while they temporarily settled in a rented high-rise condo downtown and reveled in all that a major city center has to offer. After a year or two, they were ready to begin work on their final phase home: A smallish Spanish revival style place within walking distance of the posh village center of Rancho Santa Fe, California, and the post office, charming restaurants, drug store, and coffee shops. Surely they have one of the smaller homes in this affluent zip code, but one that perfectly suits their streamlined time of life.

Finally, we worked with a brilliant 40-something computer consultant who purchased his first home upon coming back to the U.S. after years of working and living abroad in Ireland and Sweden. Single, but ready to finally settle down more permanently, he hunted for a home that might be closed up at a moment's notice. He continued working and still needed to leave for weeks at a time. He found and purchased an older unit in a smallish brick building overlooking a community park on a bluff above beautiful La Jolla Cove in the Pacific Ocean. I was hired to guide a remodel of the small two-bedroom condo. We added increased convenience with the introduction of European style under-counter washing machine/clothes dryer in the tiny u-shaped kitchen. Instead of having to hike down to the basement at odd hours to do laundry, this one change added value and convenience to his high-rise home. Because this client had the means to retrofit his older unit, he gained maximum function out of a very small space.

Shrinking the household does not mean you have to give up artwork and treasures. Built-in storage here flanks a petite fireplace and offers a cozy look. *Courtesy of Don Green – Greentree Home.*

Cooking surface and oven placed at a wheel chair friendly height. *Courtesy of Scavolini™.*

Aging Seniors

Aging is a sensitive subject. People do not want to face the negative aspects of aging and one reason might be that it isn't easy to admit that we are changing, so much so that I have found few middle age clients that will even discuss the installation of grab bars in their bathroom, a very basic safety issue for seniors. It is true that in this era we experience generally better health care and medical advances so that many people in their 70s act and look like 55-year-olds from other generations. But no matter how vibrant we think we are or how much plastic surgery one has, people in their 50s begin to experience health problems that impact how they spend the last half of life. As Boomers age, we are noticing that many people expect to work into their 60s and 70s or beyond. For some it is a choice and for others a result of the lagging economy or financial necessity. Many retire and continue to contribute to their community in a myriad of useful ways, constantly re-defining the essence of senior Americans.

Like the younger empty nesters, older Americans in their 70s and 80s often decide to sell a family home and relocate or downsize, but for slightly different reasons. Some want to move closer to a child or another relative who is involved with their daily life and can check in on them. Other seniors are moving into a single room, an accessory apartment or a portable housing unit with or close to other family members. The majority of people over age 65 who don't live in senior facilities live in some kind of a family setting. A move may involve purchase of another, smaller single family home or it may mean entering an "over 55" community. Some organized living situations offer a sliding scale of health monitoring services that is an attractive aspect for seniors with intermittent health setbacks. These apartment-like places provide meal services, social support, and some personal services too. Regardless of the many different arrangements and lifestyle changes, aging is a time of challenge and dozens of little "losses" from joint and muscle pain or weakness to waning eyesight. No one, despite their financial comfort or lack of, escapes the inevitable transformations that alter life in dramatic ways.

State of the art Italian cabinet maker Scavolini offers wheel chair accessible modular kitchens in stylish finishes. *Courtesy of Scavolini™.*

Compact kitchens are sold as a unit for granny-flats or senior apartments. This is an ADA Compliant model by Cervitor. *Courtesy of Dwyer Products Corporation.*

Basic Planning Guides for Seniors:

1. One in three adults 65 years or older fall each year. 2. For approximately 25% of the population 75 or older, falls result in serious injury (40% of admissions to nursing homes are due to falls, and falls are the sixth leading cause of death for people over 70 years of age). 3. At least one bedroom and bathroom should be located on the first floor. 4. You need conveniently located easy-to-use controls and handles. 5. Avoid throw rugs. 6. Provide good lighting everywhere for safety and good visibility. 7. Install grab bars in bathroom toilet and shower areas. 8. Use carpeting on floor surfaces rather than hard surface materials. 9. Select soft cornered and upholstered pieces vs. wood arms on seating pieces. 10. Avoid sharp glass-top surfaces. 11. Provide good color and value contrast from flooring to walls. Older people with vision problems have trouble distinguishing changing planes; they need to plainly see where floors and walls start and stop. 12. Keep floor surface on one level for easy use of canes, walkers, and wheel chairs. 13. Remove doors from bathrooms so the toilet is clearly visible and reminds Alzheimer's patients to use the toilet. 14. Consider acoustical wall coverings; some older people are sensitive to noise and it can interfere with hearing aids. 15. Provide compact kitchenettes that provide more independence from the rest of the family. 16. Modular kitchen units are made and some models comply with standards set by the Americans with Disabilities Act (ADA). 17. Budget providing, build in cabinetry can maximize storage options for seniors who move from a single family home into less space. It is very emotionally challenging to face a severe paring down of personal mementos, furniture, and artwork accumulated over a lifetime.

As people age, they often need much higher contrast between surfaces in order to see different planes. The sharp contrast between the red and white is stunning, yet appropriate for a senior resident. *Courtesy of Trend USA, www.trendgroup-usa.com*

Currently about 23% of men and women over age 65 live with relatives and another 2% live with non-relatives. Life with one's children goes smoother when the parent can retain some sense of privacy and autonomy. A granny flat, which is generally considered a room with a separate entrance and bathroom, is the ideal. However, it is important to check your local building codes that govern detached buildings before planning a separate unit. Many communities do not take a positive view on granny flats, believing that the character of neighborhoods is threatened by them. We may see specific efforts on the part of community planning groups to change this attitude as the general population ages and the need for senior housing explodes.

In other situations a parent may take over the available ground floor bedroom and displace another family member. Often major changes in the floor plan present the opportunity for broader reaching re-vamping of the entire house. Try to include the parent in the plans for their own place.

Urban 20- and 30-somethings

Young people have always been the driving force in living trends, even before the rest of a population catches up. History confirms that they are the population consistently willing to try new places and lifestyles. Around 1900, countless young Americans fled the poverty of farm life for job opportunities in newly industrialized cities of the Northeast and Midwest. From small towns in the agricultural South, where many small communities still felt the devastating effects of the Civil War, people traveled north to Chicago, Detroit, St. Louis, and New York.

At the same time, waves of new immigrants from around the globe poured into some of those same cities and others like Patterson, New Jersey, Boston, Massachusetts, and San Francisco, California. The newcomers were lured by the promise of factory jobs or even working on the new railroad routes out west. Entire families came, but there were also many young people traveling solo half way around the world in search of opportunities not available in Europe. My own grandfather, an immigrant from southern Italy in his late 20s, landed at Ellis Island and made his way west. For a while he lived in Livingston, Montana, as he worked on the railroad and eventually settled in a young Los Angeles in the late 1920s.

The mid-1930s in the U.S. and Canada were marked by another massive exodus of people from the Great Plains states to the West Coast. The so called Dust Bowl, brought about by a devastating combination of drought conditions coupled with farming habits that plowed up the grass layer of rich prairie land, was a time when the soil dried up and was turned to dust. Reportedly the dust storms that occurred were thick and the skies were black all the way to Chicago from blowing soil in places like Texas, Arkansas, Oklahoma, Colorado, Kansas, and New Mexico! Dispossessed families lived in migrant camps and were reduced to day labor in the orchards or ranches of the western U.S.

When a family could scrape together enough money, they were able to transition from living in a truck or tent, to living in a rented home closer to the heart of a city. The draw towards cities and a more hectic lifestyle was based on survival, rather than wanting the quality of city life or a particular architectural style of house. Families tried to endure intact and just lived the best that they could. The Depression Years mixed with the great Dust Bowl, and by the time the depression lifted, our nation was embroiled in the nightmare of World War II. During those war years housing was not a focus and by the time all of the men returned home, there were severe housing shortages.

The first suburbs began to appear in the Northeast as tiny houses were erected on the outskirts of major cities in response to the needs of new families. It was the first time that entire new communities were invented out of land that previously held forests, citrus groves, cattle ranches, and rich farmland. Life in these suburbs defined the 1950s and 1960s housing trends and helped to form expectations regarding housing. By the late 1950s many inner cities became overcrowded and decaying places to live. Drawn to better and innovative housing that included that latest technology and style, families fled town life for the suburbs.

An example of an early suburb remains today in the San Fernando Valley east of Los Angeles. The valley was nearly built by the Cold War aerospace industry and the entertainment industry. To this day, thousands of tiny, post World War II houses and apartments sprawl across the warm valley. The now quaint architectural styles blend together with lacy trees in a way that makes you feel as if time decided to stop in Burbank, North Hollywood, or Van Nuys. Even the shopping remains along boulevards, for the most part sprinkled with individual office buildings, restaurants, and medical buildings rather than in ubiquitous shopping malls. There are churches, mixed with old style motels, blended right next to movie studios in an odd mixture. Because this is where I was born in 1952, the valley holds an interest for me because my memories jive with what you would see today driving up and down those streets. I have motored by the house my parents lived in when they brought me home from the hospital just to check my visual memory against reality.

At the time I was born in 1952, the outskirts of thousands of cities became a destination for generations of young people who wanted a different lifestyle and a newer type of house that at the time was found in the suburbs. Two and three bedroom houses with a back and front yard, a garage that might be detached from the main structure or connected to it by a breeze-way, and a strip of green parkway next to the sidewalk. Parks, community centers, pools, and schools followed the people.

Today, in an inevitable recycling of popular lifestyle trends, our young people are more apt to want to live closer to a major city center. They are drawn by much more than just the promise of work that enticed the young in 1900. They want stylish neighborhoods packed with coffee houses, bars, restaurants, and bookstores. They want the availability of shopping and socializing all within walking distance of their abode. And, they want it packaged in a kind of sexy, fashion forward way. Most local and state governments maintain facilities downtown. High-rise office buildings are often home to regional headquarters, professional firms, and retail support businesses. Over the last ten to fifteen years, nasty commutes, congestion, and the astronomical price of gas have made living outside large cities much less desirable. Combine unhappy and blocked-up travel conditions with the extraordinarily high cost of gasoline and you'll find young people wanting to live downtown.

Cutting edge and minimal, these glass shelves provide a light look for media equipment. *Courtesy of www.Floating-GlassShelves.com.*

Retro is extremely popular with 20- and 30-some-things. Sparse look and slim lines work well in tight quarters. *Courtesy of Hunter Douglas.*

Many of the 20- and 30-year-old population are gainfully employed, but still experience significant financial challenges. Huge student loans follow those who snatch up advanced degrees as they strive to be competitive in our rapidly changing global economy. Health insurance is often either not offered as part of an increasingly shrinking or non-existent benefit package, or having it can mean a bill of over $500 a month. It should be no surprise that it is often very difficult to save for a down payment on a house in any metropolitan area. One of three things generally happens: Parents loan money for a down payment on a place that should work out for about five years; a very tiny appetizer house or condo is bought with the intention to leave as soon as possible; or the ranks of renters swell. In most cases, these "starter" houses have limited space and are generally not considered to be a lifetime home. Some can be as small as 700 square feet and serve only a single person.

Entertaining is challenging, but accessories like this 20" diameter standing beverage chiller work indoors and outdoors. *Courtesy of Smith & Hawken.*

e-Nook® Standard is a hide-away station for a computer and charging electronics at only 7" deep x 25.5" high. When opened up like a Murphy bed, it projects only 21.5" into a room. *Courtesy of Anthro Corporation.*

We watch the 20-year-olds in order to see the future for smaller spaces. In 2000, the Wear-Dated™ brand and Parsons School of Design conducted a trend study focusing on women from two of the largest consumer populations: the Boomers and Generation Y. The study, which probed the historical, political, cultural, and societal influences of female Baby Boomer and their Generation Y daughters, specifically looked at events, emerging technologies, and pivotal societal trends that shaped how a 30-year-old female Baby Boomer lived circa 1980 versus her Gen Y daughter will live when she reaches the same age in 2010. Baby Boomers used art as a youth movement to rebel against their parents' tastes with wild, psychedelic colors and intense color combinations. That trend eventually morphed into strong, rich, earthy colors such as yellows, browns, and oranges. The industrial market produced new building materials like urethane foam, fiberglass, and Plexiglas that interior designers embraced in their furniture designs. Fast-forward to 2010 and you will find that Gen Y continues to create independent styles with one dominant view rather than pluralism of expression. They will demand

multifunctional, compact furniture pieces while relying on high-quality fabrics and smooth, rounded elements of their high-tech world. A home for Gen Y might not be as spacious as their mother's first home in the suburbs was, but it will effectively serve as a modern, comfortable refuge from the urban surrounding. An important part of the interior design schemes and furniture design will include synthesized technological elements.

The main difference uncovered by this study between these two generations is the demand for high quality that is married to technology-based design flexibility by the Generation Y group. In 1980 there was enough of the hippie culture left on the two coasts to make avant-garde much more important than the quality of furniture or textiles. I had an apartment filled with plants in macramé holders and an old loveseat covered by a throw that I tucked in the corners to hide worn upholstery. To my way of thinking, I had a jazzy place. Today's twenty-four to thirty year olds want more style and cutting edge design.

Destination College

The real experts in small space living just might be college kids! Every fall a new crop of freshmen prepare to leave home and to give up rooms that are very often much larger than the little rooms they will share with strangers. Fortunately for millions of college-bound teens, the excitement of being on their own outweighs concerns over decorating their rooms. Often, this is the first time most kids have lived away from home, and there is a sense of excitement mixed with anxiety for them. The high school grads are leaving the daily control of their parents and becoming responsible for making day-by-day decisions for the first time.

Students are interested in being accepted by their peers more than anything else, so they are going to gravitate towards cool and trendy ideas on how to decorate. The room must function not only as a place to sleep, but also as a place to study, relax, and entertain friends. Color choices for bedding are probably the single most influential in determining how the room feels. There are planning guides compiled by companies like *The Container Store, Linens n' Things,* and *The Pottery Barn,* and these are available at no charge. The main lesson from residence hall living is the myriad of creative ways to stretch storage for the student: Under-the-bed in plastic boxes with wheels, pocketed hanging devices for underwear or CDs, and over-the-door hanging storage for shoes. A revolutionary way for anyone to create up to four times more storage space for extra bedding sets, sweater, seasonal jackets, etc. is with Space Bag®, the vacuum-seal storage bags. The Space-Saver Tote can hold up to four times more clothing and bedding than conventional storage boxes and bins. Parents are well advised to step back and let the student begin to make choices for themselves.

Plastic storage boxes fit under a bed to hold extra bedding and portable shelving holds everything else. *Courtesy of Container Store.*

Mobile storage caddies are great for toiletries and food supplies in residence hall rooms for students. *Courtesy of Container Store.*

Chapter Three
Dual Purpose Space and Changing Usage Patterns

Every couple of generations we notice that American families begin to use their home space in ways that are unique to their own times. This happens in direct response to particular shifts in social patterns that can cause a new type of room to be wanted or needed. For example, a hundred years ago many family homes had a receiving parlor, a place where guests waited to be announced by a butler or maid. In general an upper middle class family doesn't exist in the same format as in my grandparent's generation and we certainly don't have formal house staff any longer. People in an upper middle class designation today might be inclined to have someone come in once a week to clean, have meals cooked, have meals delivered or simply go out to eat. Only the wealthiest today would employ permanent house staff and even fewer would require them to wear a uniform. Our society does not embrace the same formalities as were standard in the 1900s clear through the 1950s. Maybe a great piece of politeness and willingness to blindly obey social rules was shredded during the tumultuous 1960s and early '70s. Not only were bras burned, but all sorts of boundaries were broken by men and women seeking to experience freedom from stereotypes.

Ethnic articles like these Winnowing Baskets from Room & Board became popular and easily accessible in the 1960s with the advent of stores like Pier One, Cost Plus Imports, and others. *Courtesy of Room & Board.*

Older homes featured a formal entry, unlike the entrance to a guest house or granny flat today. An entry door delivers you right into a living space where sense of entry can be achieved by using an area rug. *Courtesy of FLOR.*

It should be no surprise then that we can track the relaxation of rules for the home furnishing world right along with other shifts in mores, lifestyle choices, and social trends. Chaos in family structure and then society as we knew it translated into people loosening up sexually and socially. Of course they were not interested in being married to the sofa matching the loveseat, and then matching the curtains as well. Style follows society. We saw plants, many in complicated macramé hangers, becoming a part of interiors as a way to blend with nature. Organic forms and shapes became blended with ethnic design elements. When I was in high school the most exciting shopping trip was to the local Pier One or Cost Plus Import shop because it was my first exposure to items from Africa, Indonesia, Japan, and Tibet. Not only were the things that I was experiencing exotic, they were available at reasonable prices. This was the start of the shrinking world market and more ready access to products from abroad.

There was a new respect in the '60s for the handmade items, similar to the Craftsman Movement of the early 1900s that praised simplicity and crafts. Relaxation of rules translated into the popularity of hot tubs and emphasis on recreating in one's back yard that often included a wooden deck. Perhaps at this time we began to place less emphasis on the front porch and more on privacy. Textures became more influenced by the rest of the world and we saw the shag carpet, from Scandinavia, take over the living rooms of America! It was loose and comfortable on the feet. Shag carpet came in some exceptionally wild colors and stuck around for a good 30 years. It is usually flattened and faded when we find it today still in houses.

Post 9/11 it is said that the dominant trend of our times is cocooning, where people retreat to the privacy and safety of home for recreation as well as every day life. The world can barge right into our homes with astounding boldness never before known. Our challenge is more how to shield ourselves and our families from the constant barrage of rapid information and genuine global threats. There is no reason any longer for isolated homeowners to be relegated to the pages of Montgomery Ward or Sears, who furnished thousands of farm and rural community family homes across America. The Internet can deliver international styles and products to your doorstep.

The constant search for more serenity at home is why the most popular remodel project for Americans today is the bathroom. We want to reproduce a calming spa-like experience at home. This becomes a great challenge for people with quite little bathrooms. Often we try to capture part of a closet that abuts the bathroom as a way to expand an old-fashioned bathroom space. The lack of in-bedroom closet room then will be solved by a standing armoire, but the larger goal of turning the bathroom into a luxurious area is met. We see towel warmers, floor warmers, and chandeliers being used along with air-jetted tubs that allow for aromatherapy and color therapy. Homeowners want drama and comfort in the bathroom along with functional elements.

As a designer I have seen a lot of evidence over the last decade or so that people are trading in their formal living rooms for more relaxed public space in the home like a great room or family room. I converted my former family room, a room that sported a built-in bar, into a large dining room and made the formal living room/dining room combination space into my one living room. This was my way to make a smaller home function best for daily living and for occasional larger family gatherings. We surely don't need or want a wet-bar and one area for comfortable seating and television watching is sufficient.

Comfortable spots can be carved out anywhere, like this stair landing with built-in bookshelves that works as a mini library. *Interior design by Christine Brun, ASID. Photo Carol Peerce.*

In this chapter we'll look at a few smaller spaces, typically within a larger home, that represent changing uses for our own times. Areas like spiffed up laundry rooms, wrapping and craft rooms, wine rooms, or packing rooms are unique to our era. On the other hand, for people who live in really small apartments, condos, bungalows, or town houses the idea of a separate laundry room might be a laugh. There are ways to conserve space in a challenged laundry area or to make a totally new laundry spot by using a stacking unit 27" wide by 71 ½" high. Then you are able to free up the floor space previously taken up by one of those appliances. Another new invention is the tank-less water heater – originally from Japan – that can allow one to rework an existing laundry room or utility room. The elimination of a bulky water heater frees up vertical space for more storage.

The Oceanview Utility Sink from Kohler used in a multi-functional mudroom/laundry room setting. *Courtesy of Kohler.*

When you don't have room for a separate laundry room, it still is possible to get some of the features you would like. From Europe we have the idea for handy wall-mounted foldout drying racks. They can be installed near the bathroom sink or even mounted into the sides of your shower. You could get rid of your full-sized ironing board and buy a countertop variety that can be slipped into a closet or under your bed for easier storage. A good-looking trunk or ottoman might hide your ironing or mending right in plain sight in the living room. As long as the storage unit has a top, the laundry will not be offensive stored in more public space. Again, the Internet is a fabulous source for equipment that can make a little apartment function in part like larger space.

Compact design in modern version of old-fashioned secretary desk might become a home office instead of allocating an entire room. *Courtesy of Bausman & Company, Inc.*

Hidden Helper™ offers pull-out ironing board. *Courtesy of ASKO.*

Living room and work space combined. *Courtesy of Hunter Douglas.*

The home office is now as ubiquitous as television sets, but it wasn't always so. An economic recession in the early 1990s forced millions of Americans out of jobs and as a result, many began to work from home offices as they found few corporate opportunities available to them. At the same time, young mothers found that they preferred working at home in order to spend more time with their infants and toddlers. This is a slight change in habits from the young mother of twenty-five years ago, who more typically worked away from the home and invested in childcare outside of the home. She was always frazzled and unhappy with the stress of being a working mom.

Home builders of the last decade eagerly wanted to hang their hats on some different home features, and conjured up some fairly exotic new rooms to market such as "to go" rooms or "pet" rooms. The "to go" room is a space solely dedicated to storing suitcases, and packing and unpacking conveniences, while the pet rooms offer custom effortlessness for grooming and feeding of pets. Even the relationship of dog owners to their pets has changed in the last few decades. Many dog owners turn their pets into substitutes for primary relationships with humans. Marketing folks have now coined a new name for this tendency to view animals as a version of ourselves: "humanization" has blasted into the pet industry. It affects pet pharmaceuticals, food, toys, and now apparently their housing! I am the owner of two huge Labrador retriever puppies and daily at the dog park I have the opportunity to share with other pet owners. I know working people who hire pet sitters, dog walkers, and organize pet playgroups out of devotion to the dog-made-family-member! As people feel more and more isolated in our fast-paced society, pets take on a more special place in our lives and our living spaces shift to accommodate them too. I have known a client who included a small room off the living room as part of their custom designed home and it served as a well-decorated cat sanctuary separated from the main spaces by fabulous custom wrought-iron gates.

We are noticing that the old-fashioned butler's pantry is popular again, but with a new twist. It is no longer merely a place to store china and silverware. Typically a smaller area relative to the kitchen itself, modern versions of the butler's pantry add in appliances like warming drawers, dishwashers, icemakers, or wine chillers. Master bedrooms are becoming more of sanctuary space and many sport coffee bars located near the dressing area or bath so that a couple might maximize quality time together in the morning. Flat screen television technology offers a way to free up a little more space within the master bedroom or bathroom and still get the use of the TV as you dress.

Most families have at least one household computer, two or three televisions, and phones in every room. These days most everyone owns a microwave and some people have two of these appliances in one kitchen, along with ice makers, beverage centers, or under-counter wine chillers. We all have hand held phones and cell phones to be plugged in and charged over night, leading to the need for some sort of convenient place to do so. You can order a floor standing towel warmer out of a catalog or on-line, a luxury that would have been only for the wealthy 100 years ago. There are electric toothbrushes and pants pressers. Lots of households own a scanner and a fax and phone answering machines are common. These are just a few examples of small household appliances and items that we imagine we need that actually change our space requirements.

Walk-through butler's pantry leads to powder bath with space-saving pocket door. *Courtesy of Johnson Hardware.*

Butler's pantry stores wine and linens. *Courtesy of ALNO®.*

Designed for the young mother staring out, this multi-tasking laundry/ craft/ project room looks adorable, but functions in a practical way. *Courtesy of Country Home/Meredith Publishing.*

Today increased demands are placed upon a typically small room, like the laundry or utility room, that was simple in another era. These spaces are not thought of as insignificant any longer and some homebuilders bill these rooms as the command center of a household. Sometimes these rooms include a little desk, fax, scanner and telephone, gift-wrapping station, craft center, or sewing machine. We see built-in ironing boards and drip-dry closets with drains. Society now has identified the laundry room very differently from the back porch of a house built in 1935. That room might have been kind of a walk-through space with barely room enough for a utility tub and ironing board closet. We want convenience and can get it too with the right equipment for drip-dry hanging and storage.

Dual purpose space is identified as a room that must meet two needs. In small homes we find that this is exactly what creates an awkward look: The dining room must double as the home office, so how do we hide the mess when company comes? Our guest room also holds the family computer, and the kids leave their book and papers all over. How can it look like a room in a bed and breakfast? The living room must serve as the guest room on occasion and how can we make the guest feel private enough? A busy person theoretically can squeeze in the time for regular exercise if the equipment is located right in the house, but gym equipment is ugly. What do we do to conceal it?

Baby's room must also serve overnight guests and be appropriately decorated for both purposes. *Courtesy of Thibaut.*

An odd space under the stairs can be turned into a child's play area with an area rug and useful storage. *Courtesy FLOR.*

Use of space under stairs for a wine chiller and storage plus serving counter. *Interior design by Cliff Londt.*

Everyone is interested in convenience, saving time, and saving gas. The secret to successfully combining different functions in one room it to be willing to break old-fashioned "rules" about what each room ought to be doing for us. You need to be willing to shake things up a little. Each room should function to the max and this is nowhere truer than in a space-limited home.

Custom built-ins under a stair create storage and function in a space that could have gone under-utilized. *Courtesy of www.hardwoodinfo.com*

Artfully designed to force maximum function from space under the stairs. *Design by Architect Mark English.*

Dual function achieved by custom cabinet maker combines home office with home gym. *Courtesy of Hidden Grove Furniture and ICON Health & Fitness.*

Therefore we might see a little living room with four armchairs instead of a bulky sofa. The advantage of chairs is that they can be moved around easier to meet changing needs like making room for the Christmas tree or an air mattress for a guest. There are no interior design police out there. Sometimes I am not a huge fan of the HGTV channel because it falsely makes everything seem so simple to do, but it has done one very admirable thing: It took the fear away from the idea of breaking expected rules.

Making a room comply with the demands of two uses often depends mightily on flexible furniture that can perform tricks. We will examine flexible furniture and built-ins next.

Four comfortable lounge chairs replace the stereotypical arrangement of sofa and matching chairs. *Courtesy of Thibaut.*

Chapter Four
Flexible and Built-In Furniture

One of my favorite definitions of flexibility is the word *strength*. It implies that we can best get control over tiny space by being adaptable and looking at alternatives that might be a little less commonly known. If you are willing to try furniture arrangements and equipment that offer new ways to use compact space, you will increase the over-all utility of your home. It may mean throwing away your existing furniture and buying something else that has the perfect dimensions. Inches do matter in a small room, and so it is sometimes necessary to get rid of a piece of furniture if it interferes with the optimum way to use your room. You are better off to realize a mistake and try to sell it or donate it to charity than to allow a piece of furniture to impede successful function of a room. It is best if you are willing to look at your situation with an unbiased and fresh eye. Be courageous.

Multi-functional furniture is a hot commodity right now and one of my reasons for writing this book is to spread the resources around. It has been difficult for my readers to locate the items that I have featured over the last decade. So access to the right equipment is paramount. If you can get your space to serve dual functions, you have won one-half of the battle. We look for pieces that are well designed, but roll, collapse, fold, or stack. The Table Bed is billed as a "sexy" solution for small spaces by *House and Garden Magazine*, and was introduced by designer Loren Sherman at the International Contemporary Furniture Fair in 2000. Sherman, a set designer and president of the manufacturing firm Inova, was amazed at the response he got to something he originally devised for his personal use. His own friends pestered him to market this attractive and practical take on the old Murphy-style bed. His Table Bed allows one to eat, work, and sleep in the best area of a small apartment or studio. In larger quarters, use it to create a guest room in a tiny space that might double as a home office or dining area.

In "bed" mode, *Table Bed* – a unique built-in by Designer Loren Sherman – offers dual function in cramped space. *Courtesy of Inova, LLC.*

The *Table Bed* turned into a table. *Courtesy of Inova, LLC.*

Another example is from the people who brought us the original "Hydra Table," winner of the Adex Award for Design Excellence in 1997. Tired of hunching over the coffee table in his small SoHo apartment, and necessity being the mother of invention, designer Gary Gianakis decided to create a table that would raise and lower easily. His result was a glass-top table on a sleek chrome hydraulic base that allows a person to adjust the coffee table to any height – from 17 inches to 25 inches – with ease. The table also spins and can lock into place to make it easier and more comfortable to use from a seated position in a sofa or lounge chair.

With the touch of a lever the cocktail table turns into a dining height table. *Courtesy of Hydra Designs.*

A long known secret weapon for those who want to use every square inch of room is the custom built-in piece. This so called "trick" has been popular from as far back as the early 1900s. For example, you will find built-ins in Craftsman style homes with nearly each home featuring a built-in buffet in the dining room and very often built-in bookcases to separate living room from dining room. The 1950s introduced futuristic features like sliding partitions that made it possible to have either a den and bedroom or a large multi-purpose room when the sliding doors were open. Waist high planters that served as dividers from foyer to living rooms were popular. Built-in linen closets were increased and a line-up of closets dividing bedrooms from living area provided what was then considered a "superabundant storage" and it served as a sound-deadening device.

Homemaster Publications from 1957 features the work of architect Rudolph A. Matern, where one of his home offices shows a combination of cabinets with bookshelves along the top and down one side. A bed unfolds from the cabinet to convert the room into sleeping quarter. The difference today is that the home office is not reserved for business and professional men only, and women have long ago joined the work force from home. The 1950s description now seems quaint: "Whether a man works entirely out of his home or merely has occasional business callers nights and weekends, the small center bedroom indicated in the plan offers direct access from the front door through foyer and hall, thus preserving family privacy."

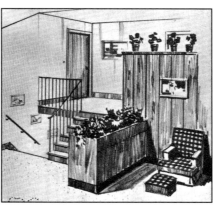

In a split-level ranch style home from the 1950s a built-in linen closet is placed behind the vertical board paneling that transitions into the waist-high planter for a glamorous entry. *Courtesy of Homemaster Publications, Inc.*

Occupying one end of a master bedroom, folding doors closed off a home office in a ranch style home of the 1950s. *Courtesy of Homemaster Publications, Inc.*

Built-in storage stolen from under a staircase maximizes available space in kitchen. *Courtesy of hardwoodinfo.com*

Shelves go up and over a window seat opening when custom built. *Courtesy of Hunter Douglas.*

Designers of small space will enthusiastically advocate the benefits of built-ins as the ultimate way to get a maximum amount of use from rooms including various odd spaces that don't lend themselves to off-the-shelf solutions. You can increase storage when you go up and over doorways, under and around windows, and beneath a staircase. Because it is becomes possible to build to suit the available area, rather than be restricted to standard sizes, custom built-ins are often a miraculous solution. You can carve out miniature shelves between studs in the walls for tiny collections. Or a carpenter might work out storage drawers under beds that are lifted to a non-standard height to suit odd items like wrapping paper and tissue, or seasonal clothing storage. People are hungry to learn about ways to stretch their space without sacrificing style and the built-in works.

The fireplace mantel and surround flow into useful, but shallow under-window bookshelves. *Courtesy of Hunter Douglas.*

Well thought out custom built-ins can look very comfortable in place while delivering matchless service to the homeowner. However be aware that built-in solutions can be expensive and so they are not the answer for everyone. When investing in the permanency of built-ins is unacceptable, an alternative can be found in dual purpose and flexible furniture items.

Another version of under-the-window shelving. *Courtesy of Hunter Douglas.*

Flexible and dual use furniture is attractive because it is more adaptable than standard furniture pieces and generally can be easily moved. Such solutions allow a room to serve several purposes because often the furniture can provide dual use. A portable screen is a perfect example. The job of a partition, whether it hangs, folds, or rolls, is to separate the mundane private areas from more public space. Another is the table that changes purpose. I've used tables that change height from cocktail table to dining table with the gentle push of a lever.

Extreme efficiency in the Unicat motor home might be copied for tightest conditions on land. *Courtesy of Avi Meyers, CEO Unicat Americas.*

Built-in becomes part of architecture by running the crown molding around the front of the unit. *Courtesy of Thibaut*

The counter expanded while cooking. *Courtesy of Avi Meyers, CEO Unicat Americas*

Dining chairs that stack enable you to store the extras in a compact space and out of sight. Anything that can be hidden away by folding up piques interest from exercise equipment that bends to beds that pull out of a wall. From the inhabitant of a one-room apartment to a happy bungalow dweller, the demand for maximum function out of every room is the battle cry.

Well designed custom dressing and closet area makes use of every inch. *Courtesy of Country Home.*

ALNO has an innovative range of swing-down interior cabinet features called *MyWay©*-designed to make access easier for a graying generation. *Courtesy of ALNO®.*

Nearly every reader who has ever written to me has wanted to know where to get their hands on a particular solution. The product section is the guts of this book. If in order to get your little kitchen to work you need a single dishwasher drawer you'll find your answer in the appliance listing. You will find the foldaway exercise equipment, collapsible bars, rolling screens, or convertible sofas.

The condiments and cooking oils move down for a person in a wheelchair to use. *Courtesy of ALNO®.*

Often the small space dweller yearns for features that are generally restricted to larger homes. One basic example is a fireplace. We tend to think that this is a bulky element not suitable for the tiny room or house. However, there are dozens of petite vent-less and self-contained fireplace units that burn safe fuels. You can move these around like a cabinet and carry them up and down stairs. There are more solid, but compact Scandinavian made wood burning stoves that are environmentally superior in how clean they burn. Another large-life feature could be a wine bar or wine cellar.

Architecturally petite fireplaces offer the same cozy attraction as larger designs. *Courtesy of Wisteria.*

At only 14.5" deep, the *Vicenza* sideboard is just 46.25" wide. *Courtesy of Ballard Designs.*

The space challenged homeowner needs to think in smaller terms, but can have a petite version combined into one cabinet with a small wine chiller, and glass storage rolled into a 61" wide x 20 ¼" deep piece. A spa-like bathroom can be designed for the smaller bathroom with careful selection of the right size tub and sink. Built-in clothes hampers, washer/dryer, or drip-dry area can also be designed into the smaller home. There is no reason to feel that just because your rooms are small that you cannot create some of the conveniences that are enjoyed in more spacious and luxurious homes.

The Vision, a freestanding, eco-friendly fireplace measuring 39" wide x 21.1" deep, which can be used as a room divider, and also comes in a 16" deep model. *Courtesy of EcoSmart Fire.*

Chapter Five
Childrens' Rooms

There is nothing as exciting as welcoming home an innocent, sweet baby. New parents have a special time fixing up the place where the little one will sleep, but often in tiny houses the newest family member may not get a room of their own right away. Don't panic, but do make an effort to create the best little space that you can. Even infants deserve the best that you can afford to give to them. A famous man once said that the best way to make children good is to make them happy and what new parent does not want the best for their infant? You can't exactly let a baby sleep in a drawer and so the space challenged parents find that creativity is required in order to make a hospitable place.

youngAmericaBaby® by Stanley Furniture offers a storage drawer for a line of baby cribs call *Built To Grow*™ making the floor space work for you. It converts in the future to toddler bed/daybed or a double bed with safety rails. *Courtesy Stanley Furniture.*

Storage drawer pulled out. *Courtesy of Stanley Furniture.*

For example, if the new baby is sharing mom and dad's room for a while, a temporary folding screen could serve as a method to divide off the bedroom. Another way to make a place for baby might be to hang a fabric from the ceiling on small rods to add softness appropriate for a newborn and create a sort of alcove. While nothing will grant auditory privacy with a baby in the same room, at least the baby will have a semblance of his or her own area and you can at least pretend that you are a little separated! Baby furniture generally comes in sweet styles and colorful bedding signifies that an infant is in residence. It is important to remember that infants need color to stimulate their eyes and even if it doesn't match the adult color scheme, give your baby that courtesy, please, in mobiles, color choices for bedding, and toys!

You might also capture the service of a closet for a time as a mini-nursery by removing the door and then making the alcove into baby-central. For many centuries, people have intuitively realized that you feel safe when sleeping in a surrounded place. Sleeping alcoves were common in Medieval Europe and in 19th century Sweden they built double bunk beds into the wall and used fabric curtains to keep the warmth inside the cubicle. For children a more heightened sense of security is always important. It is like the sense you may have experienced as a child when you made a blanket covered hideout right in the middle of the living room. You could also create a cubicle by surrounding a crib on all sides with a pliable, washable fabric. European drapery fabric is often available in 108" to 112" wide goods and is almost always washable. An interior designer can assist you in accessing such textiles.

When you share your room with your small baby, then the second bedroom in the house can be used in other ways: For a home office, guest room, or hobby room. If Mommy and Daddy take care to create a room that is soft and calm for baby, yet still offers comfort for the adults, everyone can smile. A sleeper chair, recliner or an old-fashioned rocker in the spare room can offer a place for the attending parent in the middle of the night out of earshot. A storage ottoman could hold a warm blanket, parental reading material, needlework, cross word puzzles, or coupons for clipping. Then at least one parent can get some steady and undisturbed sleep.

If you have room for a designated nursery, remember that in a small home you have to maximize the function of *all* rooms for the entire household, including a baby's room. There is no reason that the room could not double as a library or a sewing room, provided you organize supplies in a tidy way. Of course you could hide a home office in a compact office armoire and co-exist compatibly with the child's room. Or you might build in a counter height surface that can serve as a changing and dressing surface, a gift-wrap area, and craft table. It can be done with good planning and the proper equipment.

Consider soft flooring as your baby begins to crawl and take advantage of some of the fun and colorful area rugs on the market. You can un-roll an area rug and cover up less appealing carpet on a temporary basis. When you really think about it, a child's room needs to be re-vamped about every five years as your child forever grows and changes. A little kid is a precious thing and deserves to have a room that inspires, nurtures, and makes him or her feel safe. It happens so quickly that children change that most parents are unprepared for how suddenly the baby goes off to kindergarten. What is darling for an infant and toddler becomes inappropriate for a seven or eight year old kid. It is so important to be in tune with effective ways that can change the character of a room without sacrificing space or costing you a fortune.

White *elfa®* *Kids Coloring Table & Solid Shelving.*
Courtesy of The Container Store®.

Colorful *Authentic Dairy Cubes* offer a simple way to store baby clothes or supplies. *Courtesy of The Container Store®.*

Parents who live in really small homes might think carefully about how many toys and educational items, books, and play things your little one really needs to have in order to be happy. I have walked into small homes where every single room has been appropriated for the child's domain, leaving the parents kind of hungering for a more adult-colored world. By paying attention to unnecessary stuff you can make sure that everyone in the small house has as much room as possible for real needs. Be sure to sift through belongings regularly including toys, clothes, and linens.

One great idea was birthed by one Simon Horn of England who took inspiration from the 18th century's *metamorphic* furniture. Using this idea, Horn has designed a unique set of furniture that changes to match every stage of a child's development – from tiny baby to teenager. His *cot* begins as a pretty typical crib design. Then at around age 2, when the child is ready for his or her first bed big boy or girl bed, you can simply lower one side of the safety rail to get the child used to sleeping without the railing. Later both of the rails are removed. Another popular concept is to make use of bunk beds or lofts. This is a practical way to maximize free floor space for play.

8-Cube Bookcase is part of the *Cube Collection* – 28.25" wide x 13.75" deep x 57" high – with Canvas Bins offers a colorful way to organize. *Courtesy of Land of Nod.*

Part of the *Moderne* baby crib line, this crib not only offers extra storage, but grows with the child. *Courtesy of NettoCollection, LLC.*

Sarasota Striped Bench, 41" wide x 18" deep, is a sturdy wooden bench for reading and offers useful additional storage space. *Roomservicehome. com.*

There are hundreds of bed designs that pack in storage drawers, shelves, and pullout baskets. Fortunately, almost every affordable manufacturer has a plethora of furniture ideas available. American made cribs that convert into more grown up beds for toddlers are on the market. Interior designer David Netto has such a line called *Moderne* baby cribs that include toddler-bed conversion kits and linen storage boxes below the mattress.

Built-in storage offers maximum storage. *Interior design by Sherri Blum, CID, Jack & Jill Interiors.*

Interior Design by Sherri Blum, CID, Jack & Jill Interiors. Photographer Bill McNamec.

Think built-ins if you can afford it. Go up and over windows. Take advantage of all of the vertical space to build shallow shelves for stuffed animals, books, trophies, and other mementos. With limited space your mantra ought to be "organize often and purge often". Encourage your children to carefully go through their things and perhaps to give away some of their extras to less fortunate kids. Take advantage of under-the-bed storage boxes for toys and collections. If you cannot part with certain toys and books, then try to find another spot to store them outside of your house. There is no sense in taking up valuable room with out-of-date items. With all sorts of devices that hang over the door you might provide extra storage, in addition to the main clothes dresser. You can stuff underwear and socks or t-shirts in the pockets of such hangers. Alternatively, small toys might also be tucked into these pockets.

Paint and peel-off decorations called *Wall-Pops* offer an easy way to decorate inexpensively and is a temporary solution for rentals. *Courtesy of WallPops®.*

A former closet turned into an adorable sleeping alcove for a young girl. *Courtesy of Pergo.*

White *elfa® Home Business Center* offers storage for older kids. *Courtesy of The Container Store®.*

If the bedroom must also serve as a play room, once again look at fun and soft area rugs as a way to add color and give your children a plush surface on which to sit. Investigate small craft tables and cubbies that allow you to store supplies in an orderly way. It is much easier for you to look at colorful baskets than the chaos of stacked odds and ends. Plastic boxes that roll under beds are another way to gain organization for toys and books when you have limited space.

Delicate *Iron Sleigh Bed* keeps things lighter than using a wood version. *Courtesy Land of Nod.*

Washable *Pergo* flooring is practical for playrooms and a good choice for a bedroom if your child has allergies. *Courtesy of Pergo.*

This *Trundle Bed* allows for two to sleep in one room and save on floor space. *Courtesy of Land of Nod.*

Bunk bed with student desk built into one end offers efficient use of limited floor area. *Courtesy of Furniture.com Inc.*

More mature design for teenager using peel-off wall décor. *Courtesy of WallPops®.*

The *Simple Collection Bunk* can be converted to two twin beds when kids get older. *Courtesy of Land of Nod.*

Wallies wallpaper murals are pre-pasted and vinyl coated. This headboard takes up no space at all. *Courtesy of Wall Nutz®.*

Catch a wave with a tropical theme headboard pasted onto the wall. *Courtesy of Wall Nutz®.*

Do not get too invested in trying to squeeze television into your child's personal environment because experts tell us that it is not such a great idea to set up an electronic world in your child's bedroom. A survey conducted by the Kaiser Family Foundation in 2000 found that one-third of two to seven year olds and two-thirds of eight to eighteen year olds have a television set in their bedroom. By 2004 the data shows that this number continued to grow; a National Sleep Foundation poll found that 30 percent of preschoolers and 43 percent of school-aged children have a television set in their bedroom. If it is there, then the kids are more likely to spend an additional 45 minutes a day watching it, when they could be reading, playing outside, or more importantly, sleeping! It ought to be good news to parents that the American Academy of Pediatrics recommends that the bedrooms be "media-free-zones." This means not only no TV, but no computer, video games, PlayStation, or Game Boy. Many parents want to be in the same area as children working on homework, but if your home is very small, the "quiet" zone might have to be the child's bedroom.

Attic dormitory room with single wood beds, complete with clothes storage. *Courtesy of Maine Cottage.*

Shutter Bunkbeds from Maine Cottage.
Courtesy of Maine Cottage.

On the walls brush on Rust-Oleum® Specialty *Chalkboard Black* to transform any space into a play room. Paint on chair backs and on buckets to help children personalize their belongings. *Courtesy of Rust-Oleum®.*

Spiral staircase converts awkward space into a child's bedroom or play room. *Courtesy of The Iron Shop.*

Chapter Six
Living Rooms

Chances are you probably care a little more about the public rooms in your home – the ones that dinner guests or neighbors peek at upon entering your door – than what your bedroom, home office, or laundry room look like to others. We consider our entry and living room open to the outside world. There is no disgrace in admitting what is surely true for many people: We have all got rooms that we would rather not let anyone else see. It would be comforting to believe that our true friends and family do not pass judgment on what our house looks like and that we never need to worry about others visiting. But because we are human, others do make evaluations about our appearance, our houses and cars, and it can be bothersome. I will admit that over the years I have at times succumbed to worry over what others thought of my house. For everyone, home is a reflection of self and then to be an interior designer just added another heavy layer of expectations from others that I felt constantly.

The good news is that suddenly one day, wonderfully and happily, I just ceased to care what anyone else thought anymore! Call it the freedom of middle-age: The confidence to let my hair go gray, omit make-up in the morning, and get over slightly sagging body parts. However, in the interest of full disclosure and honesty, one of the reasons for my newfound satisfaction with my own home is that I did finally have the opportunity, or should we say circumstance due to a cracked slab and a burst water pipe, to re-model my entire house. This allowed for some updating of the 40-year-old house. It was wonderful to get more modern fixtures and appliances, spanking new carpet, fresh paint, and upgraded lighting. Although nothing super designer-like was done, I admit that it felt wonderful to have everything renewed.

Removable serving tray on *Tray Console* table measuring 30" wide x 18" deep x 33.5" high at entry. *Courtesy of Harden's Furniture, Inc.*

Colorful entrance with functional coat hooks and a narrow bench. *Courtesy of Valspar Paint.*

Having said that, my contentment had nothing to do with making my home larger. On the contrary, I did not add any square footage to the living room or kitchen. In fact, we did not enlarge any rooms. Why is it that I am happier now with the house that I have lived in for nearly 19 years? While the footprint of my house remains the same I made it work better for our needs. How? Before the remodel I hired my furniture delivery service to move the furniture around so that I could try out a new arrangement. It was an experiment that lasted for a few months before the remodel took off. I wanted to determine the peak wall on which to place the ever-present television. I just shook up the mix in order to find a new way to use my old space and ended up loving the results. It cost me two hours of time and under $100 to rearrange the rooms.

Very petite dining table and appropriately sized area rug make the space look larger. *Courtesy of Casuto Cottages.*

In a Levittown living room, the obligatory matching arm chairs sit stiffly in front of the picture window. *Courtesy of Levittown History Collection.*

I believe that your own flexibility as you ponder your living space is almost as critical as what furniture pieces you buy. Keep your mind open to different ways of arranging furniture. There is no truth to the concept that you have to have a sofa in the living room or need to have two lounge chairs to balance it off. First, last, and always, know that you have permission to arrange your furniture in any way that supports the room remaining pleasant and functioning.

With a fixed shelf and small drawer, this 450 Console is 50" wide x 14" deep x 35" high. *Courtesy of Harden's Furniture.*

My only caveat is that you must be willing to take a hard and realistic view of what you already own. If you have the wrong equipment, you have to be brave enough to make a change, no matter if your pieces are relatively new or not. Otherwise, it can sabotage the success and the ambiance of your room to keep something that just doesn't work. In my opinion, the inability to dump the wrong furniture is the biggest stumbling block to getting it right: We are all reluctant to admit that we've made a mistake. If something is wrong then no amount of justification is going to make it better. I am a huge proponent of cutting your losses and moving ahead.

Enter the idea of proper *scale*. Scale is a term that designers use to describe how appropriate an item is for the size of any given room. The reality is that there is no sure-fire formula for always getting it right, even though the ancient Greeks and Egyptians made a science of proportion in architecture. Going back to the Pythagoreans, there is the idea that proportions ought to relate to detailed standards. Not only has the unit of measure changed over the centuries, the idea of classical balance is not of concern to most contemporary lives. Proportion is a relative term, describing *a part in its relation to the whole.*

We like to see more petite furniture profiles in rooms with low ceilings and limited area. Avoid chunky furniture designed for "McMansions" because they obviously overpower tiny rooms. The size and shape of items used in small rooms are probably the most important characteristics to consider when making furniture selections. Somehow everyone can tell instantly when things are wrong in a room, but it's a struggle to find a way to correct mistakes with furniture or placement. Professional designers are often called in to remedy a problem when a homeowner senses that something is amiss, but can't think of how to fix the problem. Remember that while you do not have to give up grace, style, and interest in smaller rooms, you *must* analyze the situation carefully in order to get the dimensions correct.

It can help to keep in mind human scale. People average 5 feet to 6 feet in height and weigh between 100 and 200 pounds. Remember these figures as a guide as you select furniture in order to keep yourself feeling comfortable in a room – not like a giant, or midget, or "out of scale." The positive effect of some blank or negative space even in a space-starved room is also something to keep in mind as you try to arrange pleasant and balanced rooms.

Built-in window seat and shelves join with a cozy corner and day beds that are a good way to use space once popular in the 1950s and '60s. *Courtesy of Liora Manné.*

The best solution may mean that you pull the sofa right up against the breakfast bar and the room that would have been taken up with barstools is given over to an ample seating sectional instead. No one says that you must use a built-in bar as an eating surface. Or it might be that a better arrangement for you is four comfortable armchairs on casters and no sofa at all. This might enable you to easily push the chairs out of the way when you need to add the leaf to the dining table and encroach on the living room space as you entertain a group of people.

Soothing paint color swathes this room and sculptural fireplace, achieving a cozy feeling. *Courtesy of Valspar Paint.*

This narrow room uses a sleek floor tile, 118" x 47", with a highly polished finish, low media storage, and minimal vertical book storage in an elegant design. *Courtesy of Trend Q.*

Furniture pieces with legs that allow the floor to be seen is space expanding. Freestanding Euro-style fireplace and window coverings that stack up compactly also work to create openness. *Courtesy of Hunter Douglas.*

If you really want to include the warmth of a fireplace in a tiny room, your solution might rely on one of the products designed for the vent-less fireplace market. There are very narrow units that burn fuels and require no outside venting. While much more petite than a masonry fireplace, the ambiance of your room will change once you include any type of firebox. Thousands of years ago the great Roman orator Cicero said, "There is no place more delightful than one's own fireside." No one wants to give up such a feature of comfort just because the living room is small. If you are not able to physically get any type of fireplace in your room, consider the services of a good *trompe'loeil* painter who can paint the image of a fireplace on your living room wall. This will take up no room at all as it is illusion and simply paint on the wall!

Artist David Ward fashioned natural piece that takes up little space at an important front entry. *Courtesy of Sticks and Stones. Photo by Hamish Reed.*

By grouping an array of smaller items together they read as one more important unit. *Courtesy of wisteria.com.*

Little living rooms don't have to be all white in order to work in the small house. Use color effectively to build drama in a tiny area. Sometimes I paint the ceilings and all the wood trim of a room with eight-foot ceiling height pure white and the walls receive the color. Another useful trick is to paint the walls a color and then color the ceiling in 50% or one-half formula of the same color. The ceiling gets a sort of lift from these two techniques. If you have a small room with very high ceilings, then you can very comfortably swathe the entire room in color. Having said all of this, it sometimes works just as well to wrap a little powder bathroom entirely in stronger colors because the result is womb-like comfort. When you use stronger color, it is important to reduce the contrast between major surfaces and keep the material colors in similar value.

Try to avoid too much *stuff* and confine yourself to fewer and more important accessory items. You may be a collector of tiny objects: Thimbles, teacups, glass balls, or shells. Discipline yourself to arrange your collection so that it reads more as an entity. For instance, keep all of the items on one table or arrange all of them on a shelf or two instead of packing the living room landscape with things. Another great trick to keep your living room from feeling "over-stuffed" is to rotate your favorite things so that you keep very little out in public view and stash other things under the bed, in cupboards or cabinets when on reserve.

Fine furniture manufacturer makes a Pop-up with Swivel – 68" wide x 22" deep x 38" high – console that hides the actual flat screen TV when not in use. Space for TV: 41" wide x 6" deep x 28" high. *Courtesy of Bausman & Company, Inc.*

Upon entering your home, try to establish some sense of who you are right at the entrance. This does not have to take up a lot of room and can be something as simple as a narrow bench with a piece of art above or a slim table with a mirror above that says "foyer" where none really exists. A unique piece of art might hug the wall and only take up inches of depth, yet create a mood. Watch that whatever you position at your entrance does not interfere with passage into your home, but still creates a sense of entry. You might find a single interesting chair and a high, but narrow pedestal that does the trick. Or you might sit a fabulous mirror on the floor and lean it against the wall, (anchored for safety) as a way to expand an entry. A good quality area rug might be another way to establish your sense of style at the opening to your home. Don't skimp on something like this, but put time into the hunt for something that is right for your home.

Remember to visit re-sale shops as a way to purchase higher quality art, accessories, and other furnishings as very reasonable prices. Generally, they start out marking the items at one-half of regular retail value and then continue marking down over a period of a couple of months. You can always make an offer and see if the consigner will take a lower amount. I like re-sale shops also because there is such an eclectic array of styles assembled that you can never find in a store that carries just one style of furniture. It is often possible to locate much smaller sized vintage pieces of furniture that work perfectly in small homes. It's like a high-class yard sale and just like a treasure hunt! The best part is that you can find original art, nicely framed, at reasonable prices that help you to achieve a much more genuine and sophisticated look in your home. While I am not personally crazy about the thought of used upholstery pieces, if you buy an item inexpensively enough, you can afford to have it re-covered and made fresh just for you.

Perhaps one of the latest trends in living room design is the acceptance of a plainly displayed television and media equipment. With the flat screen TV becoming more affordable and available, we see that many people are tossing the bulky television armoires of yesteryear in preference of a narrow, lower cabinet that only holds media equipment. Because the screens are so minimalist and clean, an exposed TV no longer seems to stir complaints by homeowners concerned with the ugliness of utilitarian equipment. Whether in a more formal room setting or a much more casual room, this seems to be what homeowners are doing these days. The look is lighter and more minimalist, which works well in small spaces.

Chapter Seven
Kitchens and Dining Rooms

Kitchens have evolved over time into a sort of modern day hearth. No matter how small your kitchen, have you ever noticed that during any kind of gathering in your house everyone is standing in what seems like a five by five square foot area talking, munching, and enjoying each other? Food draws people together and it always will. Food preparation and consumption have been shrouded in style since the time of the ancient Romans. Wealthy families had slaves preparing meals in indoor and outdoor kitchens, and practiced ritually joyous dining. They lounged and relaxed and drank in luscious comfort. While the Roman Empire eventually fell, Italians never lost their love of good food and the place of importance eating plays in family life.

Napa restaurateur David Gingrass of San Francisco's Hawthorne Lane remodeled his own kitchen with an open island that invites gathering while he cooks.

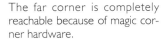

The far corner is completely reachable because of magic corner hardware.

Island storage in efficient pull-out drawers with pots, lids, and other equipment.

I know because I am pure Italian on both sides of my family and food was a huge deal! We talked about food, thought about food, and spent a lot of family time preparing food. Of course the French probably score as the most reverent people on the face of the earth when it comes to cuisine. The subject of meals is pure religion there and a very serious matter. You wouldn't be caught dead walking down a street sipping a latte and eating a bagel on the run in France. Many cultures are appalled by how uncivilized we Americans can be about dining and have disdain for our fondness of prepared and pre-packed food. It is true that there are millions of children that don't know what a real mashed potato tastes like or have ever seen their mother making homemade soup. Some of this we can blame on fast-paced lives, but some of the cause is lack of interest in the value of eating wonderfully prepared meals together as a family.

Yet, we Americans still love our kitchens like we love our cars! I've designed many kitchens for women who never cook, yet want the latest and best that the industry has to offer. In our country, kitchen design probably began in 1870 with Catherine E. Beecher and Harriet Beecher Stowe's book, *Principles of Domestic Science as Applied to the Duties and Pleasures of Home,"* which showed the ideal plan for where and how kitchen equipment should be arranged. By 1900 kitchens sported central metal worktables and freestanding wooden cupboards and cabinets.

It was not until the 1920s that mechanical home refrigeration was common and the concept of cabinets joined in various configurations came from Europe to the U.S. During the Depression, the U.S. Commerce Department proclaimed six standard colors in response to the chaos of color that previously existed regarding kitchen paraphernalia: White, Delphinium blue, royal blue, kitchen green, ivory, and red! So important was the blossoming kitchen industry that a National Kitchen Modernization Bureau was formed in 1935 to coordinate appliance manufacturers and assure continued production.

However the bureau understandably fizzled once we became involved in World War II. After the war some six million kitchens were built during 1945 to 1953, many of which are the small kitchens that have been the subject of one or two remodels by now. General Electric in a 1956 advertisement introduced refrigerators in yellow, turquoise, pink, brown, and white. These so called "mix-or-match" colors extended to fabrics, linoleum, countertops, furnishings, and smaller appliances.

There are no totally original ideas in design if you think about it. Today we see both a resurgence of the retro-colors and the old fashioned idea of pieces of furniture used for storage in the kitchen as part of cutting edge design! Even if some of us lack the dedication to the careful preparation of food found in our European cousins' kitchens, we Americans seem to love the idea of the kitchen being up-to-date.

Under-counter washing machine/dryer combination inserted into remodeled kitchen. *Interior design by Christine Brun, ASID. Photography by Jim Brady.*

UtilitySystem allows one oven to be placed at an optimum height and a small cook top angled in the corner. *Courtesy of Scavolini SPA.*

Under-counter refrigerators drawers, ice-makers, and wine chillers distill refrigeration down to the smallest package. *Courtesy of U-line.*

Often one of the first areas to receive a remodel in an older home is the kitchen and we know that such an effort can bring great satisfaction to a homeowner. In addition, realtors offer confident statistics that tell us that the remodel of a kitchen and master bathroom bring nearly 100% returns on the sale of a house. If several similar models in your area are for sale, it is a given that the house with upgrades will go faster and for a higher price. Plus, you get the enjoyment of living in an improved home during the years you are in residence. I personally place a high value on enjoying my environment at all costs, but I recognize that this is not a value that everyone can share.

The 24" wide gas cooker offers gourmet style in a small package. *Courtesy AGA.*

Built-in refrigerator with slim door that bolts right to the cabinet takes up minimal space in a motor-home and can be used to advantage in tiny kitchens. *Courtesy of Avi Meyers, CEO Unicat Americas.*

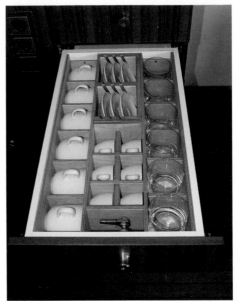

Drawer outfitted to safely store china mugs, dishes, and glasses. *Courtesy of INICAT GmbH, Germany.*

The gourmet cook does not have to be cheated out of luxury in a space challenged kitchen: There are numerous appliances that are perfect and small, but be willing to pay for the proper equipment. One example is the superb stand-alone full-functioning appliance known as the *Companion* from AGA Ranges, Inc. Measuring just 24" wide, the appliance can slide into even the smallest galley-style kitchen with four high-power gas burners and two small electric ovens, the Companion is part of the larger Aga line. Most standard ranges and cook tops begin at 30" wide. However, when used alone the unit only measures 24" wide x 23 ¾" deep x 36" high. Viking makes a 24" wide refrigerator only unit as well as the companion 24" wide all freezer. Such small dimensions are friendly to the cramped kitchen and offer flexible planning by the experts.

For the owner of the tiniest kitchens I suggest a study of nautical design and a look at how galleys are worked out. Also it would help you to scrutinize the design of the classic Airstream trailer to realize the full extent of tight planning that works efficiently in a kitchen. You will be amazed at how much function can be squeezed out of an infinitesimal kitchen in a yacht or high-end motor home! You can utilize cutting edge appliances and hardware that allow for clever planning. These days there are refrigerator and freezer drawers that might replace a more bulky appliance. We have access to dishwasher drawers and under-the-counter washer/dryer combinations that conserve space.

With the right drawer hardware you can plan to store everyday dishes and glassware in drawers under the countertop instead of in overhead cupboards. If you don't have room for upper cabinets, there is no need to feel that the space will suffer. You can make room for an 18" wide dishwasher like the Miele Incognito brand, an 18" wide wine chiller, or under-the-counter refrigerator depending upon what suits your kitchen needs. Hardware allows for things to pullout, pop-up, and flip down.

Wet bar with under-counter refrigerator and ice maker. *Courtesy of U-Line.*

For the modest kitchen, the smoothness offered by the sometimes more expensive *fully integrated* appliances is useful. These are appliances that hide the controls on the top edge of the appliance so that you don't see buttons or writing on the front of the item. I strongly advocate use of cabinet depth refrigerators and freezers as another critical way to conserve valuable inches in the kitchen. Conventional refrigerators project out into the room and make a bulky imprint. Make sure that you have no useless corners by taking advantage of Lazy Susans or magic corner hardware that enable you to pull-out the shelves from an awkward corner space.

Kraftmade™ pantry with pull-outs offers maximum use of a 24" deep cabinet. *Courtesy of Kraftmaid™.*

A good way to make use of a corner. *Courtesy of Kraftmaid™.*

Think outside the box as to how you store your canned goods, cereal boxes, and dried foods in order to achieve maximum function in your space. You do not have to plan for a walk-in pantry for maximum storage, although they are useful, if you don't have the room. There are pullout pantries and deep storage drawers that work just as efficiently.

Go up to the ceiling with cabinetry in a kitchen with an eight foot high ceiling in order to capture every possible inch of storage. Don't be afraid to put your microwave in a drawer or under-the-counter top if it loosens up the planning for the rest of the kitchen. Most importantly, design in the most convenient position for your range or cook-top, the sink, and the refrigerator. In the end the much-analyzed "work-triangle" is based on logic and your own physical dimensions.

Pots and lids organized. *Courtesy of Kraftmaid™.*

The pantry can go under the cabinets if you are short on space for the typical tall pantry. *Courtesy of Kraftmaid™.*

Both microwave and dishes can be stowed under the counter when you are short on space which is great with kids. *Courtesy of Kraftmaid™.*

A great kitchen designer will customize everything just for your habits and anthropomorphic measurements. For example, as we age it becomes more important to have one oven that eliminates the need to squat down on our knees and pull a heavy turkey out of the oven! If you have little children, it might be critical to have a microwave under the counter so that they have easy access to warming food under supervision. And in my own kitchen, my choice boiled down to placing my microwave unusually high, in order to gain a second oven at my personal best arm height. I prioritized the oven over the microwave position. There is no right or wrong in kitchen design, only the best setup for your own needs and physical reality.

Small peninsula turns into a table-height "dine-in" surface in a space starved kitchen. *Interior design by Christine Brun, ASID. Photograph by Greg West.*

Dining might have to occur right in the kitchen proper of a smaller home, but that is no reason to sacrifice the style of the dining ensemble. Built-in eating banquets allow you to conserve on floor space and still achieve attractive in-kitchen dining. The look can range from traditional to minimalist modern. Dining might have to occur at the end of the peninsula on bar chairs instead of a typical dining set. The all-important heart of any dining room is a comfortable setting in which to enjoy a meal. You need not adhere to any special "rules" in order to achieve this result. Maybe you have to work a little extra in order to pull attractive folding chairs out of a storage closet when guests that arrive are matched to the table that normally is pushed against the wall on a daily basis in order to create more room.

Condo kitchen with tiny "eat-in" table. *Interior design by Christine Brun, ASID. Photo Ed Goelich.*

Backed right up to the sink island, a built-in banquette offers good use of floor space. *Courtesy of Armstrong Cabinets.*

Built-in corner banquette and storage cupboards with shelf are features that give more functionality to this award winning kitchen. *Courtesy of Shenandoah Cabinetry.*

Dining with a fireplace in the room is an ultimate luxury. *Courtesy of Thibaut.*

Your flexibility counts just as much as the style of the furniture or the kitchen cabinets. The dining room table might be the coffee table that adjusts in height when you have people over. You just get those folding chairs out of the hall closet and set the table. Or it might be that you have to move two lounge chairs out of the living room in order to allow the dining table to expand and seat six for dinner. That's just fine and your attitude should be one of acceptance because the end result is fellowship and a good time.

Built-in banquette conserves space while oozing charm. *Courtesy of Thibaut.*

Table at cocktail height. *Courtesy of Charleston Forge.*

Table adjusts from cocktail height to dining height to perform double-duty. *Courtesy of Charleston Forge.*

Yes, it is a little more trouble to entertain in confined space, but it can be done with panache and grace. Remember, lots of fresh flowers and candles make any dining experience fun and magical. It's all about the ambiance and the food anyway, so you need to get over not having a large dining room.

Candles also work wonders to create mood and magic for dining with friends or family. *Courtesy of Colonial Candles.*

Flowers make any table setting more appealing. *Courtesy of Society of American Florists and Flower Promotion Organization.*

Three vases used with single blossoms. *Courtesy of Society of American Florists and Flower Promotion Organization.*

One basic rule to remember when entertaining is that if your home is clean and orderly, you will set the stage for a harmonious ambiance. I believe that clutter is much more obvious in the small home and visually disturbing. I cannot relax if I have guests when things are out of place. For me, it has always been a top priority to get everything clean and sparkling before inviting people into my environment. If I can gaze around my kitchen and dining room and feel satisfied then I know that I can relax into a fun meal with my family or friends. Order is not overrated when it comes to cramped houses or rooms and matters.

Built-ins attached to kitchen peninsula create mini-breakfast nook. *Interior design Christine Brun, ASID. Photograph by Jim Brady.*

Built-in display shelves in a dining room with artfully arranged treasures on shelves create atmosphere. *Courtesy of FLOR.*

Custom built-in buffet maximizes storage in an elegant design. *Courtesy of Timberlake Cabinetry.*

Chapter Eight
Bathrooms and Bedrooms

Considering that we spend a third of our lives sleeping, the bedroom as sanctuary should be a high priority when it comes to design. This is also the place where we can retreat from the rest of the household for a quiet nap or an hour of uninterrupted reading – our own little world even if the house is cramped. We go here at the end of the day to re-unite with our sweetheart. As we are wisely admonished in Ecclesiastes 4:9, II: "Two are better than one…how can one be warm alone?"

Dreamy bed enclosure is illuminated by window. *Courtesy of Wisteria.*

Practical, space-saving pull-out bedside table and storage built right into bed platform. *Courtesy of Midwest Living®.*

The boudoir in a lesser sized home very often doubles as a work space, exercise area, art studio or library. Yet, often the bedroom is one of the last rooms in the house to merit decorating dollars. Next to the hallowed kitchen, your bedroom and bathroom deserve the same reverent attention. It would be delightful to imagine that one's private area could bring the same type of serenity on a daily basis as a two-night stay at a cozy bed-and-breakfast can provide. Think for a minute: What would your perfect bedroom be like if you could design it to your personal specifications? Would it be the quietest room in the house or the one with an attached bathroom? Do you really care about a view or is an east-facing window important so you that you might watch the sunrise?

Once the uncompromising article, the bed, has been installed, most of us discover that many bedrooms are smaller than we wish. This is why built-ins are welcome additions to bedrooms along with specialty doors like pocket doors or bookcase doors that conserve the space that would have been taken up by a traditional swinging door.

Built-in to the side of the bed is papered to blend in with the room. *Courtesy of Thibaut.*

The *Box Storage Bed* offers unique secret storage space. *Courtesy of Domus Design.*

The bookcase door also allows for practical shelving for books. It is useful to include built-in shelves in a bedroom on either side of the bed if you have the room. We are interested in ways to increase storage without eating up space. Things like storage baskets under a platform bed or rolling plastic storage boxes are useful ways to increase function without taking up more space. There are Euro beds that lift up and beds that have storage drawers underneath the mattress built into the frame.

Closet hidden behind bookcase door by WoodFold. *Courtesy of WoodFold, Mfg. Inc.*

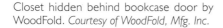

If the bed does take up the majority of your room, then how do you attain a dreamy look in your bedroom? There are ways that relate to details. First, how does light enter the room? You can select away to filter natural light from delicate fiber roman shades that sift light and allow dancing patterns through to play on walls to crisp white sheers. If you need to control light and gain privacy, solutions like wooden blinds, shutters, and mini-blinds allow degrees of adjustability that work. Lots of folks like old-fashioned fabric drapes because they brings softness to a room and can allow you to introduce pattern and color. Other people are allergic to the dust that inevitably gathers in the folds of fabric panels and thus need to look at something that draws up and down instead.

Next, take a hard look at exactly where the bed is positioned and determine if you can ignore the window placement as a way to maximize the function of your space. Why not place a bed in front of the windows so that you can get a larger size mattress in the room? It may feel like you are breaking some "design rule," but braving it opens up more options. Flexibility at work again! It might also help you out to position the nightstands or a small writing desk in front of a window without worrying about how much of the window is covered up by furniture.

Bed placed right in front of windows allows more flexibility in furniture arrangement. *Courtesy of Maine Cottage.*

Some people have no problem sleeping without window coverings. The absence brings the outside in and expands the space. *Courtesy of Maine Cottage.*

Another space-saving, but incredibly effective tool in creating mood is simple and relatively inexpensive paint. Color is probably the most significant element with influence over the bedroom. More than any other single element, the color of the bedroom can spin magic for you because of how responsive we humans are to color, both physically and psychologically. While there are dozens of web sites that offer interactive ways to "see" your room in different color combinations, I offer this hard-won bit of designer advice: Always test your paint on the walls of your room before painting the entire room. As a professional for thirty years I can swear to you that I still always test the paint that I select for myself and for my clients. No exceptions.

Try to agree on the colors used with your partner, if you have one, because it is unkind to sentence one partner to being uncomfortable in their own bedroom by swathing a room in a hue that they find distasteful. Be sensitive to the soothing quality of color and investigate soft warm tones or tranquil blues, lavenders, or blue-greens.

Headboards can eat up as much as twelve inches in depth, so another good space-saving idea is to dream up something that attached to the wall and is extremely slim in profile to take the place of a traditional headboard. By saving these inches on headboard space, you might then be able to squeeze in a bench for the foot of the bed or a small reading chair. Every inch counts and so even saving four inches in depth could prove to be very important.

Bold stripes and vibrant orange painted headboard in dynamite paint scheme. *Interior design by Karen Harris, Allied Member ASID.*

Apple green paired with coral and gold in a stunning color scheme. *Courtesy of AnnaSova.*

Wrapped in soft blue-gray paint, a slim headboard design eats up little room. *Interior design by Keita Turner. Photograph by Edgar Scott.*

Rich paisley design and hanging votives create an exotic vision of India just by using an exceptional combination of bedding. *Courtesy of AnnaSova.*

Finally, if you rent or cannot change the permanent elements, look at your bedding as another way to get some style and ambiance going without taking up any extra room. A magazine ad from Macy's once said that buying new bedding was *"like buying a new home without having to move!"* That is not exactly true, but you can add personality, color, and softness with bedding. Know, however, that you can also spend a small fortune on elaborate bed ensembles so you want to get it right. The great thing about mail-order catalog sources is that they often allow you to return the items if you are not satisfied and there are dozens of washable ideas available. Designers often provide lovely linens and custom bedcovers, but these do become costly and often are dry-cleanable only. Nonetheless, fun bedding can make a big difference in your bedroom and I recommend taking care in the selection of the coverings, shams, and decorative pillows.

Bedding in delicious colors add to the atmosphere and are portable. *Courtesy of The Koko Company.*

Every house, no matter how tiny, has a least one bath-room. We can learn much about space conservation for bathroom design by taking a look at how Europeans design bathrooms. If you've traveled, surely you have noticed that the French or Italian hotel bathroom is much smaller than our standard. I've stayed at the Club Quarters Hotels here in the U.S. and their claim to fame is that while the bathroom is very small, there is a luscious showerhead that delivers a great shower.

Block Crystal Washbasin by Lacava hangs off the wall. *Courtesy Lacava.*

Space saving Euro design creates a pull-out drawer that scribes around the plumbing to yield a usable drawer instead of wasted space. *Courtesy of Sonia America.*

Being able to see the floor beneath the fixture helps to create more sense of openness while narrow shelf offers additional surface for toiletries. *Courtesy of Valspar Paint.*

Small does not mean that you have to sacrifice quality and the Europeans have learned to hang the fixtures off the wall. This creates space below and gives the appearance of more room. Toilets and sinks are wall mounted. Instead of taking up room with swinging cupboard doors, their lavatory cabinets often feature sliding doors or lift up doors.

Tiny 48" ball and claw style tub makes romance possible in a tiny bathroom. *Courtesy of Strom Plumbing by Sign of The Crab.*

Enclosed tub makes for a more spa-like feeling. *Courtesy of Country Home®.*

There are numerous sinks on the market that are extremely small. Search for sinks that mount into the corner by design. You might consider a nine to ten inch diameter sink that was originally designed for a bar as a bathroom sink. There's no rule against that as long as the basic task of hand washing or brushing one's teeth can be accomplished. Just enough size for function is a guideline to getting a miniscule bathroom to work.

Toilet and sink in Unicat vehicle. *Courtesy of UniCat USA.*

Shower in this mobile vehicle is as compact as they get. *Courtesy of UniCat USA.*

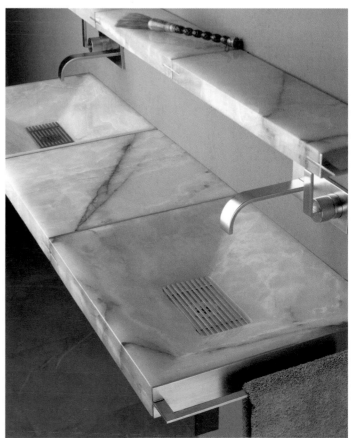

Narrow shelf above basins adds function. *Courtesy of MGS Designs.*

Limited space to mount tub filler and controls is not a problem with slim fittings. *Courtesy of MGS Designs.*

Tiny vanity snuggles into the corner with towel rings on either side. *Courtesy of Country Home.*

Custom designed woodwork sneaks in a place for hand towels just below a window. *Courtesy of Smith + Noble.*

Shortened bench at end of tub allows shared wall to become thickened built-in cubbies. *Interior Design by Tanya Woods. Photograph: Beth Singer.*

Chapter Nine
Outdoor Living and Out-Buildings

Be it ever so tiny, there is no better place to be in the spring or summertime than out in your own piece of the great outdoors. Whatever space is available to you – a narrow back porch or balcony, a squished courtyard, or perhaps a tiny yard – with good planning you can coax your area into functioning better. Outdoors spaces invite us to relax and read in a unique environment different from the inside of our homes. We are enticed to sit with a steaming cup of morning coffee, to enjoy the sound of birds, or bask in the sun with a tall, cool drink. We can get relief from a hot house by dining al fresco after the sun goes down in the summertime. Some of the most wonderful family memories for a lot of us involve eating corn on the cob and barbecue outside as the day cools off.

Hardwood interlocking exotic species tiles are removable and a good solution for renters. *Courtesy of Swift Deck.*

With only space for a couple of chairs, rockers are a romantic choice. *Courtesy of Barlow Tyrie®.*

When you decorate your outside area, think of it as a chance to be really creative and more whimsical than your interior home. You can introduce elements of nature: Stone, exotic wood, bamboo, and rocks. There are gorgeous sounds that soften the outdoors like wind chimes and water fountains. And of course plants offer hundreds of different textures and colors with which you can mold an outdoor room. Try to avoid a lot of tiny pots in an assortment of colors.

The *Outdura*™ is half an umbrella, which is good for tight spots. Extends 54" out from the door. *Courtesy of Grandinroad.*

Designed to conserve space, *The Dining Cube* allows stools to hide away under the table when not in use. *Courtesy of Veneman Collections.*

Rather, stick to one or two kinds of plant containers. Keep the pots of a good size to avoid visual chaos. It is much better to get an 18" flower bowl and plant *it* with three different bedding plants than to sit three 4" pots on the ground. They get lost and your area will begin to look junky very quickly. Please, if your plants do not do well or die over a particularly scorching weekend, replace them! Nothing is as unattractive as crisp, brown leaves of a dead plant. This does not help to establish a sense of lush tranquility and peacefulness.

The deck becomes a lush spot with right-sized potted plants and soft cushions on wicker pieces. *Courtesy of Lane Venture®.*

...ow yard includes a water feature and repetition of ...et broom plants blooming yellow. *Design Christine Brun.* ...ograph: Owen McGoldrich.*

Outdoor room established with colorful area rugs and plentiful plantings. *Courtesy of Liore Manné.*

As a designer I have noted the increased popularity over the last decade or so in outdoor kitchens and barbecue areas. These might be more challenging to accomplish in smaller spaces, but elements of the larger outdoor rooms can be achieved successfully. From small electric grills to portable ice buckets on stands, you can imitate the bigger spaces. You may have the room for some outdoor appliances such as an icemaker, or an under-the-counter stainless steel refrigerator. But if your space is limited take extra care before designing in a built-in barbecue that might be too close to the house.

Outdoor fabrics are now so soft and appealing that many families choose the for interior use because of the exceptional durability. *Courtesy of Chella.*

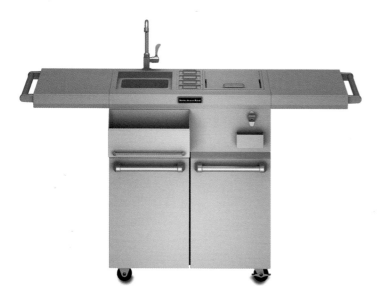

Mobile *Refreshment Center* brings water, ice, chilled beverages right to you in a 30" wide x 26.375" deep unit. *Courtesy of KitchenAid®*

If what you have to work with is a basic front porch, realize that it can be made to feel like an extension of your living room. Luckily there are dozens of sophisticated and colorful all-weather textiles on the market that are hardy fabrics. They resist fading, mildew, and rot. The fabrics made with Sunbrella™ yarns are so tough that they can be cleaned with bleach. Lovely, all-weather sheers are on the market, available through interior designers, and can help to screen off a balcony or porch area. Outdoor fabrics soften the outdoor spaces, but in addition are very practical when used inside in family rooms or dining rooms.

Stunning colors in outdoor textiles. *Courtesy of Laurie Bell.*

Another useful thing to remember as you prepare your outdoor space is safety from West Nile Virus. There are many things that you can do to contain mosquito infestations, starting with cleaning up any mosquito breeding sites in your neighborhood or yard. Because these pesky insects don't care about fences, it is important to work with your neighbors. A rather stylish mosquito curtain is available on the market that can be custom designed to fit any area. It attaches using a choice of Velcro or a sleek aluminum tracking system similar to those used for hospital privacy curtains. Hang the curtains from March till September then remove, wash, and store them for the next season.

Look for the same flexibility that we explored for indoor function when buying outdoor furniture. We treat our patios, terraces, and decks to be extensions of our homes-places to retreat to and play in, to relax and entertain guests. Again, you can find items that folds, stack, roll, or collapse for easy storage. If you live on the coast, hunt for furniture made of lightweight, but super-durable aluminum. You will be grateful because they will endure from year to year in the salt air. From rolling ice chests to slender collapsible bars, there are cool items available that will increase the function of your space. Chairs stack. Dining tables fold up and away. Fire pits roll. There are even a myriad of washable outdoor carpets available that you can literally hose off! Lighting can create dreamy space at very little cost. Remember candles need to be monitored and sheltered from the breeze. A host of decorative twinkle lights and mini-lanterns are also widely accessible at reasonable costs. You can even use your leftover Christmas lights in order to create ambiance. Outdoor floor and table lamps are now made that operate by battery and eliminate any awkward cords. From citronella spikes to sun activated pathway lights, you have dozens of ways to light the outdoor room.

Mosquito protection can be adapted to all outdoor spaces. Removable, washable, and attached with a choice of Velcro or aluminum tracking system similar to hospital privacy curtains. *Courtesy of www. MosquitoCurtains.com*

Stacking *Equinox Chairs* conserve storage space. *Courtesy of Barlow Tyrie.®*

14' x 16' *Palmerston Guest Cabin. Courtesy of Summerwood Products.*

A prefabricated 10' x 12' structure is used here as a home office detached from the main house. *Courtesy of Courtesy of Bruce Damonte.*

Pre-fabricated out-buildings have been around in Europe for a long time and their popularity here in the U.S. is beginning to climb. In England they have long used little huts or sheds with a lot of style as garden outposts in the yard. In Scandinavia they have kits for outdoor sauna rooms, some feature bathrooms too. Little buildings that come in kits might be used as playhouses, a home office, a guest room, or an artist's studio. With the fall of housing prices, many homeowners who once dreamed of trading up might have to find new ways to make a smaller house work.

Prefab modules can be constructed anywhere. *Courtesy of Modern Cabana.*

Staying put in your home could be easier to accept if you can get the space to function as you need it to work. There are dozens of companies (like MetroShed, Modern-Cabana, Shelter-Kit) that offer pre-fabricated home offices. There are many that offer charming, single room huts in varying styles from a replica of a Vermont sugar cabin to a little Victorian structure. These generally require that you pour a slab. If you are interested in such an addition to your property, check your local building codes to make sure that you will be in compliance with regulations. In my city, if the structure is less than 100 square feet, you do not have to pull a building permit. Obviously, you also need to run electricity to the structure and air conditioning or heating, as you desire.

Gibralter model kit. *Courtesy of JamaicaCottageShop.com*

Cottage might serve as guest quarters, studio, or home office. *Courtesy of Summerwood Products.*

My favorite example of good design in a small package is the "Katrina Cottage" devised by a young Greenwich Village architect named Marianne Cusato. When the horrible hurricane Katrina hit the Gulf Coast states, the devastation left thousands homeless. The call went out within six weeks to groups of architects and designers to design innovative ways to meet the needs of the displaced with dignity and was based on the infamous FEMA trailer. Trailers range from 200 to 400 square feet and Cusato's design for alternative shelter won her the Smithsonian Institution's first People's Design Award in October of 2007. Her cottages were so popular because they retained charm and appeal while being all of 544 to 936 square feet. She retained elements that people traditionally love, such as wood windows, front porches, picket fences, and wood siding. While designed originally as replacement shelter, Marianne Cusato's elegant designs are also options for seniors to young families wrestling with affordability and lifestyle issues. They might serve as a guest cottage to a much larger home as well.

Other architects are taking neighborhood cottages a step further and making them to resist future storms, dry rot, and mildew. Ocean Springs architects Bruce Tolar and Michael LeBatard have designed a cottage to fit into the local vernacular. Another prototype developed by Home Front Homes in Englewood, Florida, is built to survive being completely submerged in water. After a flood, one would remove the furnishings that have been wet and hose down the interior, and replace electrical switches. The house is built with panels sandwiching cement boards and polystyrene foam and can withstand 140 mile per hour winds. Building technology being used in Holland, where the sea is a constant threat, include homes that are built to float and are connected to utilities via a flexible conduit. Clearly these small structures have a big future all over the world.

Cusato cottage was designed as replacement housing for Hurricane Katrina victims and is intended to be added to incrementally as finances allow. *Courtesy of Lowe's.*

A unique prefab floating sauna building is the brain-child of Ari Leinonen, an architect who was born in Sweden to Finnish parents. For the Finns, saunas are a way of life, a bathing custom that has survived for around 2,000 years. When I first came across this information, I had to write about his houseboat-sauna. *SeaSauna* comes fully assembled or as a kit which you can order with or without pontoon-like attachments, enabling the building to float gracefully in water. For the 200 square foot model it starts at around $30,000. Would this building style be of use for Americans that live along rivers prone to flooding year after year? The future of pre-fab seems wide open as architects and engineers think outside of traditional constraints.

SeaSauna is a floating sauna that comes prefab in a kit or fully assembled. It can be purchased with pontoon-like attachments. *Courtesy of CIA Stiernstedt/ssark.*

Clad in alder wood, the sauna is available in three sizes. *Courtesy of CIA Stiernstedt/ssark.*

Built with a glue-lam type structure that resists the rigors of water and steam. *Courtesy of CIA Stiernstedt/ssark.*

A view of the sauna room. *Courtesy of CIA STiernstedt/ssark.*

Finally, the ultimate in unusual small space living has to be the converted garbage truck from Europe that sells for an astounding $841,348 euros! Called the UNICAT, this vehicle was designed for the serious trekker and can go anywhere as an all terrain 6x6 machine. It includes an outside connection to city water, an outdoor shower, and mosquito netting. Amenities inside rival any high-end motor coach in the world: Freeze-proof drinking water tanks, radiant heat in the living area, and a central vacuum. Comforts of home also include a porcelain toilet, hydraulically operated motorbike rack for two motorbikes, a stove with an oven, and a built-in espresso maker mounted to the wall above the sink. With built-in knife and dish storage, the kitchen looks like any state-of-the-art home kitchen in Europe. The asking price assures that this is the definitive toy for affluent Boomers.

Interior reveals an interior that is similar to nautical design. *Courtesy of Avi Meyers, UniCat Americas.*

Dining and sleeping quarters. *Courtesy of UniCat GmbH, Germany.*

The all terrain truck called UniCat is the ultimate adventure vehicle. *Courtesy of Avi Meyers, UniCat Americas.*

Chapter Ten
Product Guide

This book was written because I discovered that there is nothing like it on the market: One place that collected all of the resources useful to small space living. I wanted to give my readers details about good suppliers and contact information. As a columnist, I was not allowed to promote or to report on specific products. Without being able to share with my reader information about how to actually purchase the equipment that makes small space living better, I felt that I was not doing a complete service to my readers. "If you have built castles in the air, your work need not be lost. That is where they should be. Now put the foundation under them," said Henry David Thoreau. This chapter, I hope, will be the foundation for many households and make the job of outfitting small homes easier.

Appliances

Acme Kitchenettes Corporation
www.acmekitchenettes.com
info@acmekitchenettes.com
800-322-4191
Compact kitchens of quality and dependability. ADA compliant kitchens.

AGA Appliances
www.Aga-appliances.com
The Companion- 24" wide dual fuel range in 15 Euro colors and *BlueStar*- 24" wide four-burner gas range.

Ariston
www.aristonappliances.us.com
ariston-usa@indesit.com
Refrigerator drawers and extra quiet washer/dryer combo unit.

ASKO
www.Askousa.com
Ultra Care Drying Cabinet, Hidden Helpers – pullout shelves for folding laundry, ironing board, *Combination Washer/ Dryer* model ASKO WCAM1812 for tight quarter, no ventilation required.

Compact kitchen Model CK30-1 with a refrigerator is 30" wide x 25" deep x 39.5" high. *Courtesy of Avanti Products.*

Mini Kitchen is a tiny convection oven and two burners. *Courtesy of Avanti Products.*

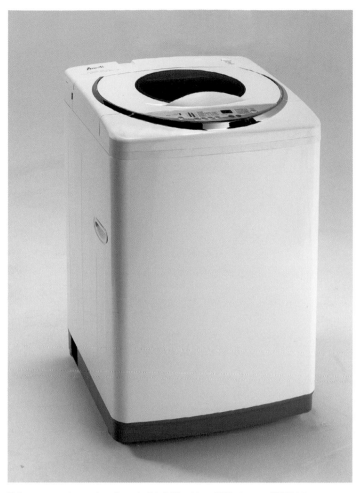

Fully automatic washer is only 21.25" wide x 22" deep x 37" high. *Courtesy of Avanti Products.*

Bosch has an 18" wide dishwasher that is known to be the quietest around. *Courtesy of BOSCH Home Appliances.*

Avanti

www.avantiproducts.com
800-323-5029
Compact to apartment size refrigerators 24" deep, freezers, wine coolers, microwave ovens, gas and electric ranges, laundry products, mini kitchens.

Big Chill

www.bigchillfridge.com
info@bigchillfridge.com
303-444-4050
Retro refrigerator design in eight colors.

Bosch

www.boschappliances.com
800-921-9622
212-966-7183
Kitchen Architecture -System 20: Freestanding stainless steel components on casters.

DeLonghi

www.aga-appliances.com
12" Gas cooktop
DEGCT212FX
12" Electric cooktop
DEECT212F

Dwyer Products

www.dwyerkitchens.com
800-822-0092
Dependable compact kitchen units.

Compact wet bar sold as a unit. *Courtesy of Dwyer Products.*

Northstar is a 1950s retro range with 21st century insides. *Courtesy of Elmira Stove Works.*

Dishwasher drawers from Fisher & Paykel offer the option to place the drawer at optimum height for a senior. *Courtesy of Fisher & Paykel.*

Elmira Stove Works
www.elmirastoveworks.com
800-295-8498
50s Retro appliances with 21st Century insides.

Equator
www.equatorappliances.com
800-776-3538
Energy efficient combo washer/dryer

Fisher & Paykel Appliances Inc.
www.fisherpaykel.com
888-936-7872
Dishwasher drawer units.

Frigidaire
www.frigidaire.com
800-374-4432
18" wide dishwasher-Model FMB33ORGC

Gaggenau
www.gaggenau.com
617-255-1766
Modular cooking units good for small kitchens.

GE Appliances
www.geappliances.com
800-626-2000
Profile 18" wide dishwasher.

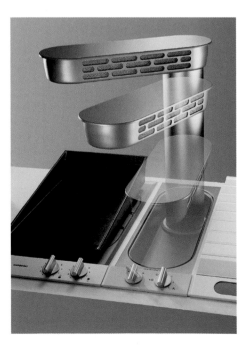

Gaggenau's VL 051 *Telesc Swivel Ventilation System. Courtesy of Gaggenau.*

20.6 Cu.Ft. Counter Depth French Door/Bottom Mount offers a slim freezer drawer that can be an energy saver. *Courtesy of Haier.*

Haier
www.haier.com

Refrigerator with unique 4 door design, ability to convert compartments from freezer to refrigerator; under cabinet wine cellars, washing machine/dryer combo. Largest manufacturer in the world of refrigeration. Portable counter-top dish washers in fun colors: Sea Gree, Red, Passion Pink, Autumn Orange.

Kenmore
www.kenmore.com
18" wide Portable dish washer- model 17259
18" wide dishwasher- model 14403

KitchenAid®
www.kitchenaid.com
KitchenAid Satisfaction Center
800-422-1230 (Major appliances)
800-541-6390 (Countertop appliances, kitchen appliances)

10-Single-Drawer Dishwasher offers Whisper Quiet® Sound Insulation System. *Courtesy of KitchenAid®.*

Dishwasher drawers offer more layout options in a kitchen. *Courtesy of KitchenAid®.*

48" wide SBS2415 *Side-by-Side* combination unit offers a wine cabinet with two zones in Euro-cabinet depth style. *Courtesy of Liebherr Appliances.*

18" wide dishwashers are good for wet bars, coffee bars in master bedroom, butler's pantry, or a granny flat. *Courtesy of Miele.*

Liebherr
www.liebherr-appliances.com
Extremely quiet units, 24" deep x approximately 22" wide, fully integrated units, freezers, wine chillers.

Marvel Industries
www.marvelindustries.com
800-428-6644
Refrigeration: Drawers, wine chillers, sinks.

Maytag®
www.maytag.com
New, slimmed-down Maytag® *Centennial*(™)-27-inch dryer fits through doorways and into small laundry rooms. Standard dryers are commonly 29" wide and washers are about 27" wide.

Miele Appliances
www.miele.com
800-843-7231
G818SCVi slimline dish washing unit 17.75" wide x 24" deep; ovens, cooktops, dishwashers, vacuums, washer/ dryer combo units.

PB Teen
(Pottery Barn)
www.pbteen.com
866-472-8336
Supercool Fridge 19" x 19" x 19 1/5"
Tiny refrigerator with freezer in navy, orange, or pink.

Perlick
www.perlick.com
800-558-5592
Stand alone 24", 48", 72" stainless 34.25" high refrigerators, freezers, wine chillers, refrigerator and freezer drawer units

Sailor Sams
www.sailorsams.com
877-230-7353
Tappan Space Saver compact dishwasher 17 3/8" wide x 21 ¼" high x 19 ½" deep

Sharp® Electronics Corporation
www.sharp.com
Cooktop and microwave drawer combo

Sub-zero Freezer Co., Inc.
www.subzero.com
800-444-7820
Freezer and refrigerator drawer units

Takagi
Takagi-usa.com
888-882-5244
888-882-5244 Corporate Headquarters
Tankless water heater

Tankless water heater – the *T-K3-SP* – is perfect for residential use at 13.8" wide and only 40 pounds. *Courtesy of Takagi.*

Under counter refrigerators open up more counter space. *Courtesy of U-Line.*

Thermador®
www.thermador.com
1-800-656-9226
24" wide refrigerator columns and freezer columns, 18" wide and 24" wide wine preservation wine columns.

Freedom™ Collection fresh food columns 24" and 30" – freezer columns 18" and 24". *Courtesy of Thermador®.*

U-line Corporation
www.u-line.com
414-354-0300
Small ice makers, wine captains under-counter refrigerators, freezers.

Viking

www.viking.com

24" wide gas range has four burners, a convection oven and an infrared broiler.

VGIC245-4B-Gas 24" wide four-burner *companion range*. *Courtesy of Viking.*

Whirlpool

www.whirlpool.com

Washing machines, dryers, laundry euipment.

Wine Enthusiast

www.wineenthusiast.com

800-356-8466

Winestar and *Slim-Line* models and variety of space saver wine cellars.

Bathrooms

American Standard

www.americanstandard-us.com

Distributes Porcher models that are suitable for tight spaces such as the *Angle Wall-Mounted Corner Handbasin Kit, Sapho Wall-mounted Lavatory,* and *Novella Wall-Mount Lavatory.* Also American Standard *Corner Minette Wall-mount Sink. Walk-In Bath 26" x 51".*

Crate & Barrel

www.crateandbarrel..com

Rotation mirror storage tower.

Design Within Reach

www.dwr.com

Modern furniture in stock and ready to ship; *Bellavista* dressing room mirror designed to close by Carolo Marelli and Massimo Moteni; *Quovis* stanless steel cabinets by Italian restaurant supply.

Duravit USA, Inc.

info @usa.duravit.com

770-931-3575

Pee Wee fixture collection just for toddlers. *Courtesy of GERBER.*

Gerber® Plumbing Fixture

www.gerberonline.com

866-538-5536

PeeWee™ Collection

Tiny kid-sized lavatories and toilets with lower mounting heights; smaller bowls with 10 1/8" rim height.

Hammacher Schlemmer & Company, Inc.
www.hammacher.com
800-321-1494
48" diameter x 36" high Japanese soaking tub/stainless steel ringed with Asian bamboo.

Home Decorators Collection
www.homedecorators.com
800-245-2217
Wicker storage collection; small traditional wood sink cabinets; kits for flexible storage pieces.

Hooker Furniture
www.hookerfurnitue.com
T.V. consoles, shoe cupboard, home office, bedroom

Aquamedia Double Washbasin in compact form. *Courtesy of Lacava.*

Tiny *La Dolce Vita* wall mounted sink. *Courtesy of Kohler®.*

Kohler®
www.kohler.com
800-456-4537
Tellieur™ Series storage furniture; *Purist*™ Series storage furniture; *Marston*™
Wall-mount corner lavatory; *Sonata* Corner Shower; *Undertone*™ under counter narrow sink modules; *Greek*™ Bath whirlpool under 5 feet; *Mayflower*™ Bath – cast iron corner bath; *Freewill*™ bath & shower barrier free modules.

A way to achieve separate basins, yet retain compact footprint. *Courtesy of Lacava.*

Lacava®
www.lacava.com

Lasco Bathware
www.LASCOBathware.com
Gardenia I – 54.25" wide x 41.125" deep small tub with integrated step

MGS Designs
www.mgsdesigns.com
561-218-8798

MTI Whirlpools
www.mtiwhirlpools.com
MTI Whirlpools
670 N. Price Rd.
Sugar Hill, Georgia
Antigua, MDTD-75 – 59.5" long x 35.5" wide x 21" high; small freestanding bath with clean lines built of Lucite® cast acrylic and reinforced with fiberglass/resin titanium
Recipient of the 2004 KBB Product Innovator Award.

Diamond shaped *Neptune* tub saves space. *Courtesy of Neptune.*

Neptune
www.neptuneb.com

Premier Bathrooms
www.premier-bathrooms.com
800-578-2899
Small safety walk-in bathtubs for physically challenged.

The *Novella Wall-Mount Corner Lavatory* is 28.5" across and 25.375" deep.

Porcher
www.americanstandard.com

Robern®
www.robern.com
900-877-2376
Unique storage vanity medicine cabinets with integrated lighting and electrical outlets.

Sonia America
www.sonia.com

The *Julien Bathroom Suite* offers a petite Japanese-style soaking tub 55.125" x 55.125", Tansu chest 35.25" x 23.375" in a combination of stainless steel and teak. *Courtesy of SONIA.*

Strom Plumbing by Sign of the Crab
www.signofthecrab.com
916-638-2722

Topdeq
www.topdeq.com
U.S. Office: 866-876-3300
Fax: 866-876-3301
Flexible bath-turn, the *Brew Macchiato Coffee Cabinet*,
Coffee Express Crema Coffee Cart, *Side-car* collapsible
serving cart, mobile drawer carts by Antonio Citterio
& Olivery Loew.

Vintage Tub & Bath
www.vintagetub.com
877-868-1369
Exclusive 48" long claw foot tub and 54" model.

Waterworks
www.waterworks.com
800-899-6757
Petite washstands, classic porcelain pedestal lavatories,
baths storage cases
*Palladio Junior Pedestal, Pier Small Vanity, Opus Single Vanity,
The Pier Collection, Boulevard Crystal* leg washstand.

Westelm
www.westelm.com
Modular storage units.

The *Panorama* is a 42" x 42" square cast iron shower pan good for a corner. *Courtesy of Strom Plumbing by Sign of the Crab.*

Cabinetry

ALNO®
www.alno.com

Armstrong Cabinets
www.armstrong.com

At only 4' long, *The Harmony* cast iron tub will fit anywhere. *Courtesy of Strom Plumbing by Sign of the Crab.*

Narrow pull-out pantry could fit into a cramped space. *Courtesy of Bulthaup.*

Bulthaup
www.bulthaup.com
newyork@bulthaup.com

Crown Point Cabinetry
www.crown-point.com

KERF Design, Inc.
www.kerfdesign.com
206-954-8677

KraftMaid™ Cabinetry
www.kraftmaid.com

Scavolini
www.scavolini.com
Universal design modular kitchen cabinets.

Shenandoah Cabinetry
www.shenandoahcabinetry.com

Timberlake Cabinetry
www.timberlake.com

Design Professionals

Mark English, Architect
mark@markenglisharchitects.com
415-391-0186

Karen Harris
EFF.ESS Studios
info@effess.com
330-351-5423

Cliff Londt
cliffnsdc8@yahoo.com

Keita Turner
KT Design Solutions
212-348-9784

Tanya Woods
XStyles
www.xstlesbath.com
248-544-3850

Surface mounted industrial-style hardware allows a heavy door to slide.
Courtesy of Bartels.

Doors and Windows

Bartels®
www.bartelsusa.com
866-529-5679
Exceptional doors and fine architectural hardware made in Germany.

CTT Furniture
www.cttfurniture.com
858-587-9311
7034 Carroll Road
San Diego, CA 92121
Traditional Japanese shoji sliding doors.

Fenstermann Insektenschutz
i.scholz@fenstermann.com
619-665-9446
Unique and patented track-free screen door made in Germany.

Häfele

www.hafele.com
800-423-3531
Fax: 800325-6197
Sliding wood door fittings, sliding glass door fittings, pocket door hardware, *ProPocket™* Door System for retractable doors, pivot sliding door fittings.

Johnson Industries

www.johnsonhardware.com
Excellent pocket and sliding door hardware made in the USA.

NanaWall® Systems, Inc.

www.nanawall.com
800-873-5673
Folding door systems and individual sliding systems.

Shoji Designs, Inc.
www.shojidesigns.com
253-857-4712

The Sliding Door Company™
www.slidingdoorco.com

100

Velux®
www.velux.com

Built into the angled ceiling a compact home office made more appealing with natural light and creative collage of art. *Courtesy of Velux.*

Woodfold Mfg. Inc.
www.woodfold.com
503-357-7158

Closed, the *Bookcase Door* looks like any other set of bookshelves. *Courtesy of Woodfold Mfg., Inc.*

Able to support up to 500 pounds, the system opens smoothly and quietly. *Courtesy of Woodfold Mfg., Inc.*

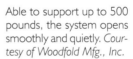

Bookcase Door allows an ordinary passageway between rooms to work for you. *Courtesy of Woodfold Mfg., Inc.*

Exercise Equipment

The Bowflex® Revolution™
www.bowflexrevolution.com
Home exercise gym, portable folding, rolling home exercise
gym with SpiraFlex® technology.

Brookstone
www.brookstone.com
800-351-7222/800-846-3000
Fold-Away™ Treadmill
Fold-Away™ Cardio Stepper
Fold-Away™ Elliptical Strider

DayBreak Fitness
www.daybreakfitness.com
Mini Stationary Bike – Fits under a desk
Stamina 15-0200 InTone Folding Recumbent Bike
Confidence Foldable Stow Away Exercise Bike

Hammacher Schlemmer
www.hammacher.com
800-321-1484
The Fold-Away 39 Exercise Gym folds to 42" long x 28" wide
x 8" deep to slip under a bed or to store in a closet.
The Foldaway Recumbent Exercise Bike folds into 42" h
x 25" wide x 19" high

The *Foldaway Recumbent Exercise Bike* folds into a
compact 42" high x 25" wide x 19" long. *Courtesy of
Hammacher Schlemmer.*

Nordic Track
A division of ICON Health & Fitness
media@iconfitness.com
888-308-9620
Fold-away gym furniture.

Sears
www.sears.com
Sears National Customer Relations
800-349-4358
Folding exercise equipment.

Smooth Fitness
www.smoothfitness.com
Smooth 5.45 Folding Treadmill

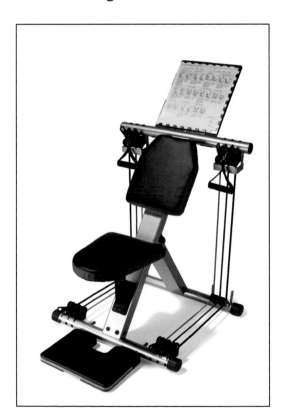

The *Fold-Away 39 Exercise Gym* weighs only 45 lbs.
and folds easily to store under a bed or in a closet.
42" long x 28" wide x 8" deep folded. *Courtesy of
Hammacher Schlemmer.*

Nordic track folding exercise equipment. *Nordic Track*

Fireplaces

Buck Stove®
www.buckstovecorp.com
828-765-6144
Model 18, 21, 80, and 81.

OptiFlame® — 35" high x 23.5" wide x 1.5" deep profile — is ideal for condominiums, lofts, apartments, or single homes as it plugs into any standard 120V outlet or may be hard-wired. Courtesy of Dimplex North America Limited.

Dimplex
www.dimplex.com
800-686-6663
Electric wall mounted firplaces.

EcoSmart's *Retro*, inspired by the 1960s, is 34.64" wide x 22.87" deep x 34.56" high. *Courtesy of EcoSmart™.*

EcoSmart® Fires
www.ecosmartfire.com
1-773-278-4100
Burner sold separately for custom design; burns denatured ethanol; sleek small scale contemporary designs can be used as space divider.

Heat-N-Glo
www.heatnglo.com
Paloma™ Freestanding Gas Fireplace sleek European fireplace 18.875" w x 15.875"
Twilight™ II ventless see through double-sided fireplace.

Hearth & Home Technologies, Inc.
952-985-6000
Tiara Petite zero clearance gas stove.

Hot Art
www.hotart.co.za
Artist Alex Kielczynski
Freestanding ceramic fireplace like a portable Mexican pottery chiminea; a signed piece of art; raku and decorated glazed ceramic fireplaces from Capetown, South Africa.

Heat & Glo offers European-styled *Paloma®,* 18.875" wide x 15.875" deep x 40.75" high, a freestanding gas fireplace with tall firebox, perfect for viewing from bed-level. *Courtesy of Heat & Glo™.*

KozyHeat® Fireplaces
www.kozyheat.com
800-253-4904
Two Harbors fireplace 18" wide x 32" high x 14.5" deep.

Montgomery Ward®
www.wards.com
Stafford

Two Harbors Direct Vent Gas fireplace is 19.5" wide and 33" high.
Courtesy of Kozy Heat.

Napoleon®
www.napoleonfireplaces.com
800-461-5581
Direct vent gas fireplaces.

Rais & Wittus
www.raiswittus.com
914-764-5679
State of the art non-catalytic burn technology from Finland; clean, modern designs and small scale models.

Spirit Elements
www.SpiritElements.com
800-511-1440
Cheshire corner design, *Metro* and *Whistle*.

Stafford
www.homevisions.com
Ventless Portable Fireplace

The *Tureen*™ GD82-T direct vent gas fireplace shown with Napolean's exclusive stainless steel surround.
Courtesy of Napolean Quality Fireplaces.

A corner welcomes the *Freemont Corner Fireplace.*
Courtesy of Sunjel.

Vent-free *The FireStage Series. Courtesy of Vermont Castings.*

Sunjel™
www.thesunjelcompany.com

The Victorian Fireplace Shop
www.thevictorianfireplace.com
866-GASCOALS
Tiny combination mantels and surround in
cast iron totally non-combustible 38.25"
high x 29.25" wide x 2.25" outside
depth/ shelf depth 5.5".

Vermont Castings
www.vermontcastings.com
Fireplaces.

See through fireplace for two rooms inside and out by Vermont Castings, *Chateau
See-Through* is the first type to be sealed well enough to be considered as a window.
Courtesy of Vermont Castings.

Furniture

Ballard Designs
www.ballard.com
800-536-7391
Multiple storage items, kitchen islands, and buffet/
wine storage.

21.5" wide x 18" deep *Beadboard Entry Cabinet*.
Courtesy of Ballard Designs.

Compact *Hampstead Island*, 65.75" wide x 24" deep.
Courtesy of Ballard Designs.

Covington Bench, 33" wide x 12" deep. *Courtesy of Ballard Designs.*

37" diameter *Piedmont Kitchen Island* with butcher block
top. *Courtesy of Ballard Designs.*

Bausman & Company

www.bausman.net

Secretarial, Computer Work Station, Flat Panel Pop-up
  Swivel Cabinet.

Broyhill Furniture Industries, Inc

www.broyhillfurn.com

800-327-6944

Computer armoires, entertainment cabinets, bookcases,
  sofa tables, and dining tables.

#6083 in the opened position with pullouts and room for everything.
Courtesy of Bausman & Company, Inc.

Compact home office #6083 closed looks like a bank of drawers. *Courtesy of Bausman & Company, Inc.*

Take off of an old fashioned secretarial #6664. *Courtesy of Bausman & Company, Inc.*

In the opened position, this modern secretarial stores everything you need for a home office. *Courtesy of Bausman & Company, Inc.*

Carlyle

www.carlylesofa.com
973-546-4502
The Chameleon 112" wide sectional sofa bed with queen size sleeper turns into a side-by-side chaise lounge, ottoman and armless chair.

Cassina USA

www.CassinaUSA.com
800-770-3568
Mackintosh Gateleg Table, *La Barca* folding table by Peiro De Martini, *Juno* bed, *Ghiretto Ghiro* bed.

The sofa that changes shapes—*Chameleon*.
Courtesy of Carlyle Custom Convertibles.

Chameleon in long format. *Courtesy of Carlyle Custom Convertibles.*

Century Furniture

www.centuryfurniture.com

Barcelona sideboard offers two pull-out bread boards as a way to expand the usefulness. *Courtesy of Century® Furniture.*

Barcelona with bread board in use. *Courtesy of Century® Furniture.*

Charlston Forge
www.charlstonforge.com

Conde House
www.condehouse.com
Delia round table with drop edges that forms a 51" square.

Crate & Barrel
www.crateandbarrel.com
800-323-5461
Wentworth Desk 52" w x24" d compact closing desk.

DWR (Design Within Reach)
Sliding Sofa, Bingo Pouf, Cubits, Archimedia Laptop.

Hi-Lo Pasta Table goes from cocktail height to dining height. Courtesy of Charleston Forge.

Domus Design Center
181 Madison Avenue
New York, NY 10012
212-685-0800
8806 Beverly Blvd.
Los Angeles, CA 90048
(310)273-5050
Box Bed/storage bed.

Frontgate
www.frontgate.com
800-626-6488
The *AeroBed Raised Headboard Bed* close to the real thing —inflatable twin or queen size beds.

Gordon International
www.gordoninternational.com
800-446-9872
Pamplona Series stacking arm and armless chair, Classic *Jacobsen* stacking side chair designed c.1955, *Sophie* Stackable Arm chair, Classic *Gateleg Table* design 1918 by C.R. Mackintosh.

Grange Furniture
www.grange.fr
310-659-7898 Los Angeles
212-685-9057 New York
Traditional French styles, kitchen furniture, Campaign style collapsible pieces, small vitrine, TV stand, corner cabinets, small bar cabinets, iron and wood small wine rack, trolley.

Greentree Home
www.greentreehome.com
800-643-6223
Studio furniture maker Don Green.

Gump's of San Francisco
www.gumps.com
800-284-8677
Red Lacquer Console Table 36" w x 10" d x 35" h.

Hammacher Schlemmer & Company, Inc.
www.hammacher.com
800-212-1484
Folding furniture, folding & very sturdy European room service table.

Hardin's Furniture, Inc.
www.hardinsfurniture.com

Howard Miller®
www.howardmiller.com
616-772-7277
The Wine Cellar 28" w x 20" d x 40.25" h cabinet on wheels for wine, liquor and glass storage and lift off top tray for serving. *Rosé Console* with two wine drawers for 18 bottles, small wine refrigeration unit, glass storage 22.25" w x 20" deep x 22.5" h.

A clever way to hide storage is the *Box Bed* shown closed. *Courtesy of Domus Design Center.*

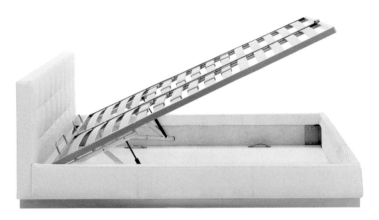

The open *Box Bed* reveals the storage compartment. *Courtesy of Domus Design Center.*

Hydra Designs
www.hydradesigns.com
Original *Hydra Table* has a standard height adjustment range of 17" to 25" high. Wheels are an option so table can be moved around easily. *Hydra TV* stand.

IKEA®
www.ikea-usa.com
Well priced and designed furniture from kitchen cabinets to storage to bedroom and living room pieces.

Adjustable height *Hydra* table goes from cocktail height to dining height with the touch of a hydraulic pump. *Courtesy of Hydra Designs.*

Inova™
www.inovallc.com
Unique custom *TableBed* with built-in bookcases – pull down that alternatively becomes a dining table or a bed. *Captain's Bed* with super drawer system.

Eloquent fold-away *TableBed* in dining mode. *Courtesy of Inova LLC.*

TableBed turns into a comfy bed. *Courtesy of Inova LLC.*

Captain's Bed with *Super Drawer System. Courtesy of Inova LLC.*

JC Penny Corporation
www.JCPenney.com
Sleeper sofas.

Jennifer Convertibles
www.jenniferfurniture.com
800-JENNIFER
Nationwide chain of sofa bed stores.

Land of Nod
www.landofnod.com
800-933-9904
Babies, toddler's and kid's furnishings and accessories.

Ligne-Roset, USA
www.ligne-roset-usa.com
Crescendo© Convertible table with a choice of heights – plus top pivots 90° then unfolds to double the surface area transforming cocktail table into a dining table.

Maine Cottage
www.mainecottage.com
Bunk-beds, trundle beds, shelving, cabinets, baskets.

Murphy Bed Company, Inc.
www.murphybedcompany.com
800-845-2337
Manufacturer of folding wall beds.

Napa Style
www.napastyle.com
866-776-1600
Numerous small wine storage pieces.

NETTO Collection
www.nettocollection.com
Stylish baby furniture.

The *Cabriolet Wine Cabinet* opens to reveal prep area and offers wine storage at 33.5" wide x 18.5" deep x 41" high. *Courtesy of Napa Style.*

Palecek™
www.palecek.com

Good use of a corner with the *Monterey Triangle Ottoman,* 32.5" wide x 23" deep x 18" high. *Courtesy of Palecek™.*

Flexible *Hudson Upholstered Ottoman* acts as seating and coffee table with each piece, 20.25" long x 25.5" wide x 20" high. *Courtesy of Palecek™.*

Pier 1 Imports
www.Pier1.com
Small cabinets, tables, chairs.

Pottery Barn
www.potterybarn.com
www.pbteen.com
www.potterybarnkids.com
Hundreds of affordable upholstered pieces, casegoods, bedroom furniture and children's furniture. Storage equipment, entertainment pieces and bathroom storage units.

Precident Furniture
www.precedentfurniture.com
Bunching tables, round tripod table, swivel chairs.

Restoration Hardware
www.restorationhardware.com
Sleeper sofas

Room & Board
www.roomandboard.com
Sleeper sofas, extension tavles, shelving, kids' furniture, bunkbeds.

Rowe Furniture
www.rowefurniture.com
Small sized sofa beds/ offer blow up mattress.

Sauder Woodworking
www.sauder.com
Computer bureaus and armoires.

Sligh Furniture Company
www.sligh.com
Home office furniture and small sized desks.

Stanley Furniture
www.stanleyfurniture.com
276-627-254

The Container Store®
www.thecontainerstore.com
888-266-8246

This End Up®
800-605-2130
Bunk, beds, trundle beds and small.

Topdeq

www.topdeq
866-876-3300
Unique contemporary furnishings from the European office market such as rolling and collapsing card, *Macchiato Coffee Cabinet, Gordon Chair, KitCase* mobile mini kitchen
Kit and Caboodle fold-up mini kitchen.
Gastone folding service cart.

Wesley Allen

www.wesleyallen.com
Sheraton Daybed with trundle bed.

westelm

www.westelm.com
Bathroom modular furniture, entertainment pieces, rolling storage, beds, slim metal headboard, flexible furniture.

Wisteria

www.wisteria.com

Wood Brothers Furniture Ltd.

www.oldcharm.col.uk
International Tel: +44 1920 469241
U.S. Office:
866-466-4747
Tudor style English oak reproductions made in UK; small scale pieces including cabinets, bookcases, desks, side boards, computer bureaus, dining furniture corner video cabinets, and bar cabinets.

Hardware

Blum

info@blum.com
Hinges, drawer and pull-out systems, assembly devices for furniture, cabinetry, and space saving devices.

Häfele America Co.

www.hafeleonline.com
336-889-2322
Hinges, cabinet decorative hardware, drawer and pull-out systems, assembly devices for furniture, pop-up tables, fold-down beds, slide-out cabinet doors, etc.

Johnson Hardware

www.johnsonhardware.com
800-837-5664
Exceptional quality pocket door frame kit and hardware.

Company Kids®

www.thecompanystore.com
Anti-tip Kit

Kitchenettes

Acme Kitchenettes

www.acmekitchenettes.com
800-322-4191

Avanti

www.avantiproducts.com
(see appliances)

Modular Storage works in bathroom setting. *Courtesy of WestElm.*

Compact mini-kitchen is easy to insert in a former closet. *Courtesy of Dwyer.*

Dwyer
www.dwyerkitchens.com
800-822-0092

Unique and elegant compact kitchen from Habersham, fine furniture maker. ©*Habersham Plantation Corp.*

Habersham
www.habershamdesigns.com
800-HABERSHAM

Pressalit, Ltd.
www.pressalit.com
Pressalit Care® Indivo Kitchens compact kitchens with height-adjustable lifts for physically challenged individuals.

Topdeq
www.topdeq
866-876-3300
Kit and Caboodle fold-up mini kitchen and *Kit Case* mobile mini kitchen.

Laundry

Ariston
www.indesit.com

ASKO *UltraCare*™ drying cabinet. *Courtesy of ASKO Appliances, Inc.*

ASKO
www.Askousa.com
Ultra Care Drying Cabinet, Hidden Helpers-pullout shelves for folding laundry, ironing board, Combo washer/dryer WCAM1812.

ASKO *Combo WCAM1812* is only 23.5" wide. *Courtesy of ASKO Appliances, Inc.*

Pull-out shelf in ASKO's *UltraCare*™ offers efficiency in laundry room. *Courtesy of ASKO Appliances, Inc.*

Gladiator®
www.gladiatorgw.com

Hide-A-Way Ironing Boards
www.hideawayironingboards.com
800-759-4766
Ironing boards that store against closet walls.

Iron-A-Way®
www.ironaway.com
Fold-away and built-in ironing boards.

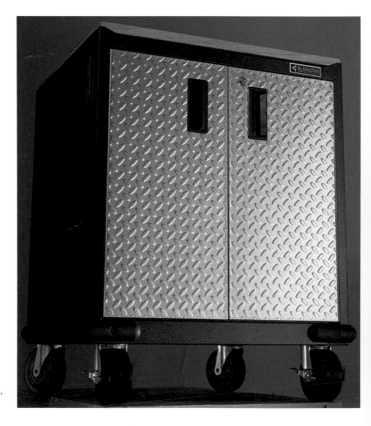

Rolling stainless steel *Gladiator*® Garageworks cabinet, 28" wide x 25" deep. *Courtesy of Whirlpool.*

Kohler®
www.kohler.com

Laundry Room Organizers
www.containerstore.com
800-733-3532
*Accordian Drying Rack, elfa® Laundry Center,
iron organizer.*

Maytag
www.maytag.com

Whirlpool
www.whirlpool.com
*Compact 22" wide LCE4332P top loading.
Under countertop or stacked 24" wide LHW0050PQ
frontloading.*

Gilford sink is 24" wide x 22" deep. Courtesy of Kohler®.

Side by side washer/dryer partially hidden by sliding cabinet. Courtesy of Maytag.

Media Centers

Bausman
www.bausman.net
Pop-up media cabinet.

Pop-Up with Swivel – 68" wide x 22" deep x 38" high – offers room for a TV measuring 41" wide x 6" deep x 28" high. Courtesy of Bausman.

Low media console units. *Courtesy of bell'o.*

Bell'o International Corporation
www.bello.com
Home theater and plasma TV furniture.

Broyhill Furniture Industries, Inc.
www.broyhillfurn.com

Cassina USA
www.CassinaUSA.com

Design Within Reach
www.dwr.com
800-944-2233
Lula Collection designed by Luis Vidal in wenge
	wood and aluminum for media equipment.

E-Nook
www.anthro.com
E-Nook wall mounted compact computer station

Slim-fit *E-Nook* work station hangs off wall and is only 7"
deep when closed. Open, the unit is 21.5" deep x 25
5" high x 36" wide. *Courtesy of Anthro®.*

Patented shelving uses a tongue and groove system that eliminates the
need for frames or hardware. Allows minimal look for hanging TV, CD
player, and collectibles on shelves that hold up to 100 pounds per shelf.
Courtesy of FloatingGlassShelves.com.

Floating Glass Shelves
www.FloatingGlassShelves.com
8000-679-4902

Gump's San Francisco
www.gumps.com
800-284-8677
Hana Sideboard 63" w x 19" d x 31.5" h, *Quattro Entertainment Cabinet* 50" w x 20.5" d x 66" h. *Stepped Tansu.*

Harden's Furniture
www.hardensfurniture.com

Mobile TV cart that rises and lowers by hydraulic lift.
Courtesy of Hydra Designs.

Hydra Designs
www.hydradesigns.com

Hooker Furniture, Inc.
www.hookerfurniture.com

IKEA®
www.ikea-usa.com

Lederer Studio
ledererstudio@yahoo.com

Philips Electronics
Us.philips.com

Pottery Barn
www.potterybarn.com

Team HC
www.teamhc.com
High end oriental screens to hide plasma TVs

The Container Store
www.thecontainerstore..com
elfa®Solid Shelving

Custom made TV and media equipment console by Tom Lederer. *Courtesy of Lederer Studio.*

Modular media storage equipment. *Courtesy of WestElm.*

Room & Board
www.roomandboard.com

West Elm
www.westelm.com

Eli Wilner & Company
www.eliwilner.com
High quality frames for plasma screen TVs.

Woodwind Media Hutch is modular and allows you to design what storage you need. *Courtesy of Room & Board.*

Miscellaneous

AnnaSova
www.anasova.com
877-326-7682

Chella
www.chellatextiles.com
805-560-8400
Luxurious outdoor + high traffic textiles.

Colonial Candles
www.colonialcandles.com
866-445-9993

FLOR
www.flor.com
8656-281-3567

Hunter Douglas
www.hunterdouglas.com
800-789-0331
Window treatments.

Liora Manné
www.lioramanne.com
Furniture, area rugs, lighting, home accents.

Pergo
www.pergo.com
Flooring with zero clearance available at Home Depot and
    Lowe's.

Rust-Oleum®
Chalkboard Black paint45

Smith+Noble
www.smith+noble.com
Window treatments.

The Company Store
www.thecompanystore.com
Anti-tip hardware kit.

The Koko Company
www.kokotrends.com
718-392-7799
Bedding, pillows and children's specialty items.

Thibaut
www.thibautdesign.com
800-223-0704
Wallcoverings.

Trend Group USA
www.trendgroup-usa.com
Contemporary porcelain tile.

Valspar Paint
www.valsparpaint.com
800-845-9061

WallNutz®
Wallpaper for kids.

WallPops™
Peel off decorations for the wall.

David Ward, Artist
520-265-6282
Sticks and Stones

Music Systems

Bang & Olufsen America, Inc.
www.bangandolufsen.com
Beo 9000 sleek wall mounted system
Beo Center 1 and 2

Bose®
Bose®Wave®Music System – compact stereo/CD player
Bose®Acoustic Wave®

Popio™
www.popiotray.com
Popio CD Tray is an innovative pop-up CD storage designed
    to fit standard letter size file cabinets, desk drawers and
    most bookshelves.

Sony
www.sony.com
800-222-SONY
Manufacturers of "mini" entertainment & audio systems.

Out-Building Designs

Jamaica Cottage Shop
www.jamaicacottageshop.com
802-297-3760
Cottages, potting sheds, doll houses, traditional Vermont
    Sugar Shack, outhouses, bath houses, etc.

10' x 12' *Florida Room. Courtesy of Jamaica Cottage Shop.*

Katrina Cottages
www.katrinacottages.com
www.casutocottages.com

Loew's Katrina Cottage Series
www.loews.com

Developed in response to a disaster, the Cusato Cottage incorporates wood windows and a charming front porch into a little footprint. *Courtesy of Lowe's.*

Loftcube
www.loftcube.net
420 square foot to 588 square foot loft cube designed for rooftops and transportable by helicopter to urban settings!

MetroShed
www.metroshed.com
310-295-0072

Modern Cabana
www.moderncabana.com
515-206-9330
Modern pre-fabricated structures.

Modern Living
www.modernliving.se
SeaSauna by Ari Leinonon

Polehouses.com
www.polehouses.com
808-478-6329

Portal Market
www.portalmarket.com
Modern teepees with heating and cooking facility.

SeaSauna
www.modernliving.se

Shelter-Kit
www.shelterkit.com
603-286-7611
12' x 12' modular shell

Spirit Elements
www.SpiritElements.com
800-511-1440

Summerwood Products

www.summerwood.com
800-663-5042
Garden sheds, cabins, gazebos, workshops, pool houses.

A 10' x 12' *Copper* Creek model cabin home. *Courtesy of Summerwood Products.*

Sweetwater Bungalows

www.swbunglalows.com
P.O. Box 9684
Truckee, CA 96162
800-587-5054
Prefabricated & portable tent-cabins,
    semi-permanent and affordable.

The 14' x 16' *Palmerston* model guest cabin.
Courtesy of Summerwood Products.

The Cool House Plans Company

www.coolhouseplans.com
800-482-0464
Plans for little homes from 574 to 1,250 square feet in a traditionally charming style. Gives regional costs to build individual plans in low, medium, or high interior finish range.

Tipi.com

www.tipi.com
541-389-3980
Authentic Native American tipis.

Unicat Americas

www.unicatamericas.com
415-515-6644
All terrain vehicle for rescue, escape, survival, or pleasure.

Outdoor Living

Ballard Designs

www.ballarddesigns.com
800-536-7391

Big Green Egg

www.biggreenegg.com
Big Green Egg Mini Heavy Duty Grid Grill 9.5" grill, ancient clay "kimado" style cooker

CB2

www.cb2.com
800-606-6252
Grasshopper Chair folding plastic weave

Char-Broil Patio Caddy

www.charbroil.com

30" Café Table and Folding Chairs. Courtesy of Ballard Designs.

Decking Tiles
www.thedeckingoutlet.com

Interlocking patio tiles come in Brazilian hardwoods and are removable. *Courtesy of Decking Tiles*

Frontgate.com
800-626-6488

Contempo patio table with storage shelf below. *Courtesy of Frontgate.com*

Glouster
www.gloster.com
Accessories Collection® designed by Povl Eskildsen
Portable insulated *ice box*© Model 229 -35.5" wide x 25.5" deep x 28.5" h
Bristol 28.5" diameter teak table, *Bristol* 35.5" square teak table, *Bristol* Gateleg table,
Bristol folding teak tables.

Folding teak *Weston Dining Table. Courtesy of Gloster Furniture.*

Mobile ice chest. *Courtesy of Gloster Furniture.*

Grandin Road
www.grandinroad.com

IPR Hardwood Tiles
www.hardwoodhome.com
888-335-8453

KitchenAid®
www.kitchenaid.com
Freestanding Refreshment Center 64.5" wide on casters with
AquaSense™ 500-gallon water filter, ice bin, cold food
storage compartments, cutting board, sink and faucet,
bottle opener and cap catcher.

Kohler®
www.kohler.com
Undertone® Trough Basin K-3154 - 22" long x 8.25" wide x
5.25" stainless steel basin.

Lane Venture®
www.laneventure.com
800-235-3558
High end wicker and rattan outdoor furniture.

Folding Bar folds down from 48" wide x 17" deep x 40" high into an amazing 3.5" so it can be stowed at the end of your porch or balcony. *Courtesy of GrandinRoad.*

Magma Gas Grill
www.magmagasgrill.com
Del Mar gas grill 18.25" base with a 16.25" diameter grill
x 41" high

Petite *Del Mar Grill. Courtesy of Magma Products.*

Mosquito Curtains
www.mosquitocurtains.com

A front porch is safely captured as living space by using a mosquito curtain. *Courtesy of Mosquito Curtains.com.*

Palecek
www.palecek.com

Storage is easier with the *Patio Terrace Chair* and takes up less space with stacking chairs. *Courtesy of Palecek™*.

Smith & Hawken
www.SmithandHawken.com
800-776-3336
Garden sheds, furniture, and accessories.

Sturdy *Cedar Hutch* is 36" wide x 28" deep x 74" high. *Courtesy of Smith & Hawken.*

Portable 30" diameter *Backyard Firepit* can make any space cozy. *Courtesy of Smith & Hawken.*

Folding teak chairs, 17.5", and a small 29" diameter table, called *Sienna Dining* set. *Courtesy of Smith & Hawken.*

Prefabricated fireplace and chimney is only 31" wide x 26" deep and 77" high. *Courtesy of Smith & Hawken.*

Swift Deck
www.swiftdeck.com
866-206-8316

Hardwood squares clip together and turn a
balcony into a warm living space. *Courtesy of
Swift Deck.*

The Iron Shop
www.TheIronShop.com

Spiral staircase allows space-saving and safe access
to an outdoor area. *Courtesy of The Iron Shop.*

The Veneman Group
www.Venemanfurniture.com
Outdoor and patio furniture.

Barlow Tyrie, Inc.
www.teak.com
856-273-7878
Plantation grown teak furniture.

Screens and Wall Dividers

3-form
www.3-form.com
Baker, Knapp & Tubbs
www.bakerfurniture.co

Contemporary accordion-like screen *Parametere* in apple green. ©2007 – 3form, Inc.

128

Century Furniture
Articulated Mirror Screen by Kelley Hoppen modern room divider is an adaption of an antique Japanese screen.

Corsican Furniture
www.corsican.com
213-749-7851

Crate & Barrel
www.crateandbarrel.com
Jackson folding screen

CTT Furniture
www.cttfurniture.com
7034 Carroll Road
San Diego, VCA 92121
858-587-9311
Custom shoji screens by Japanese trained furniture master craftsman.

Design Within Reach
www.dwr.com
Ricci Room Divider wood slat design.

Gump's of San Francisco
www.gumps.com
800-284-8677
Firori Six-Panel Screen- Hand-painted in old-master style96" w x 84" h.

HermanMiller
www.hermanmiller.com
Eames Molded Plywood Folding Screen by Charles and Ray Eames six u-shaped sections each 10 inches long; the screen unfolds to 60 inches long and just 2.25" thick.

Hightower
www.hightoweraccess.com
Folding Screen designed by Eileen Gray in 1930 with wooden frame and two differing perforated panels in high-gloss lacquer black or gray.

Horchow
www.horchow.com

Modern *Articulated Three Panel Mirror Screen.* Courtesy of Century® Furniture.

Mirrored panels open space up. *Courtesy of Century® Furniture.*

Sliding *Skyline™ Gliding Window Panels* may be used as a room divider as well as window coverings. *Courtesy of Hunter Douglas.*

Hunter Douglas
www.hunterdouglas.com

Palecek
www.palecek.com
800-274-7730
Split rattan three panel screen and Bamboo coco curtain

Pro-Med Products
www.promedproducts.com
Privacy screens on high strength 1" tubular steel frames with white vinyl curtains that could be changed. Model 313, 340 and 342.

Stickley
www.stickley.com
315-682-5500
One Stickley Drive
Manlius, New York 13104

Target™
www.target.com
Well priced folding screens in variety of style options.

Topdeq
www.topdeq.com
New Public rolling library shelves.

Unica Home
www.unicahome.com
Kraft Paper Softwall by Molo, *Cartooms Screen* from Baleri Italia is a 13-foot length of corrugated paperboard that can be arranged in any configuration you like. Part of the permanent collection at the Museum of Modern Art! *Fiore Partition Wall* by Zanotta expensive laser-cut steel intricate leaf pattern.

Warisan
www.warisan.com
877-warison
Portable coco screen.

Wesley Allen
www.wesleyallen.com
800-303-2050
Wrought iron daybeds and trundle beds.

westelm
www.westelm.com
800-937-8356
Flexible furniture, rolling storage, modular bath furniture, storage tables, organizers, baskets, beds, dining tables, upholstered pieces, slim metal headboard, narrow display shelves.

Williams Sonoma Home
www.wshome.com
888-922-4110
Kent Trolley vintage library cart, *Montgomery* multi-level table.

Senior Resources

www.aginginplace.org
Websites provide information on design ideas, useful products and how to find them, and professionals who can help homeowners plan and implement home modifications.

Cupboards that slide up and down. *Courtesy of ALNO®.*

In lowered position. *Courtesy of ALNO®.*

Dishwasher at accessible height. *Courtesy of ALNO®.*

Alno®
Universal design modular kitchen cabinets.

American Ramp Systems
www.americanramp.com
800-649-5215
www.barrierfree.org

Concept 360°™ personal design & planning
www.concept360.com
970-221-4334

Elcoma
www.elcoma.com
Flip Up Safety Rails

Home Care® by Moen®
www.homecare.moen.com
SecureMount™ Anchors allow for mounting grab bars securely anywhere without hitting a stud or arranging for new blocking behind the drywall. Available @ Lowe's, Manards, Ferguson, Ace Hardware and Do-It-Best.

Pressalit Ltd.
www.pressalit.com
Pressalit Care® Indivo Kitchens- Compact kitchens and cooking units with height-adjustable lifts suitable for people with physical challenges from the UK.

Roll-A-Ramp
www.roll-a-ramp.com
866-883-4722
601 West Main Avenue
West Fargo, ND 58078
Roll-a-ramp two piece roll up ramp weight just about 26 lbs, gives wheelchair and scooter users portable access to vans & buildings.

Scavolini
www.scavolini.com
Universal design modular kitchen cabinets.
www.seniorsafehome.com

Spiral Staircases

Affordable Spiral Stair, Inc.
www.stairwaybuilders.com
623-581-9211
2313 W. Adobe Drive
Phoenix, AZ 85027
Offer a *unistair* i.e. precision welded together into one sturdy unit.

Spiral Stairs of America, Inc.
www.spiralstairsofamerica.com
800-422-300
Affordable steel, wood or aluminum construction.

Spiral stair case kits allow access to another floor without taking up as much room as a traditional staircase. *Courtesy of The Iron Shop.*

The Iron Shop
www.theironshop.com
800-523-7427

York Spiral Stair
www.yorkspiralstair.com
800-996-5558
Harwood with no center post in 5 foot, 6 foot, 6 feet inches and 18 feet.

Storage and Organization

Alno®
Euro-style modular cabinets.

Pullout shelves allow for easier access to lower storage areas. *Courtesy of ALNO®.*

Better drawer organization enables more storage capacity in little room. *Courtesy of ALNO®.*

Ballard Designs
www.ballarddesigns.com
800-536-7391

Bed, Bath and Beyond
800-Go-Beyond
Accessories and storage equipment

Brookstone
www.brookstone.com
800-926-7000
Organizers for golf bags, shoes with carpet bottom, bike stands, workbench, 12" wide single locker, storage cabinet on dolly.

California Closets
www.californiaclosets.com
800-873-4264
Custom closets.

The Container Store®
www.thecontainerstore.com
888-266-8246

Floating Glass Shelves
www.floatingglassshelves.com
800-679-4902
Sleek and minimal mounting of glass shelves.

Get Organized®
www.shopgetorganized.com
800-803-9400

Colorful storage boxes can be left in plain sight. *Courtesy of The Container Store®.*

Mini slide-out desk and two upper drawers for supplies in *Billplayer Cabinet*, 24.25" wide x 15.25" deep. *Courtesy of Ballard Designs.*

Large translucent stacking drawers and fabric magazine pockets help organize. *Courtesy of The Container Store®.*

Cubes and rectangles, *Ladoro Shelving* is flexible polypropylene.
Courtesy of The Container Store®.

Metro® Commercial Garment Rack.
Courtesy of The Container Store®.

Extra wide at 60", the *Metro® Commercial Office and Media Center* comes with 5" wide industrial casters.
Courtesy of The Container Store®.

Pink and white *Juxta* drawers on legs, *Juxta* drawers on casters, and *Large Nested Woven Nylon Bins* for storage.
Courtesy of The Container Store®.

Juxta drawers, blue and white. *Courtesy of The Container Store®.*

Gladiator®by GarageWorks
www.gladiatorgw.com

IKEA®
www.IKEA.com
800-434-4532
Shelving, modular storage systems & storage equipment.

Hold Everything
www.holdeverything.com
800-421-2264
Specialty hangers, storage equipment, shoe racks, closet organizers, shelves and drawers.

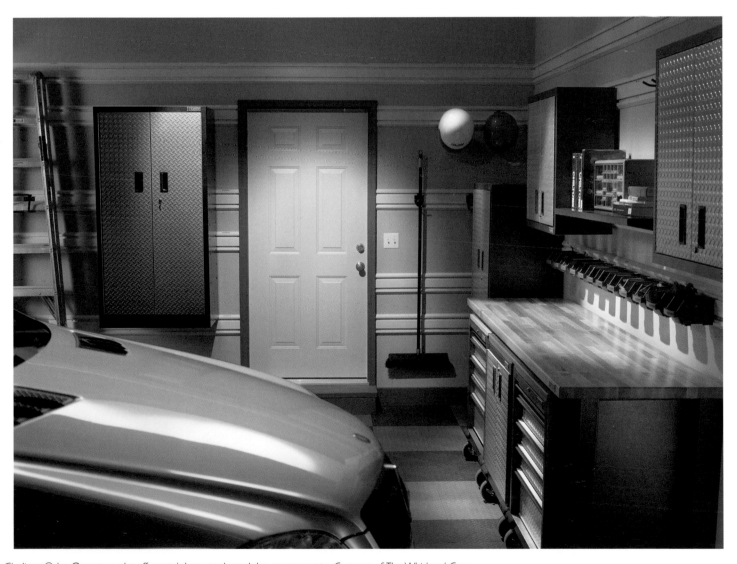

Gladiator® by Garageworks offers stainless steel modular components. *Courtesy of The Whirlpool Corp.*

Kraftmaid™

www.kraftmaid.com
Harmony™ Storage Solutions
Organizing hardware and drawers for kitchen, garage, bath, home office, and laundry rooms.

Linens 'n' Things

www.lnt.com
866-568-7378
Yaffa storage systems

Pottery Barn

www.potterybarn.com
800-922-9934
Holman Collection Bottle Shelf - 24" w x 10" d and *Glass Shelf* - 24" w x 10" d.
Ellis Storage Cube - 18" square storage ottoman, *Stratton Collection* bed with drawers below mattress for storage, *Caleb Flat-Panel TV Stand* - 55" x 14.5" x 74.5" with storage for CDs and books.

Maximum pull-out efficiency doubles the amount to be stored. *Courtesy of Kraftmaid® Cabinetry.*

Pantry goes under the counter with special hardware. *Courtesy of Kraftmaid® Cabinetry.*

Storage of pots and lids. *Courtesy of Kraftmaid® Cabinetry.*

Rubbermaid®
www.rubbermaid.com
330-264-6464
Closet kits, shelving units, plastic containers, garage storage.

SmartFurniture®
www.smartfurntiture.com
888-467-6278
Smart Organization - stylish storage units 9.5" deep, *SmartCubes™*.

The Closet Factory
www.theclosetfactory.com
800-692-5673
Custom closet systems.

The Container Store
www.thecontainerstore.com
elfa® garage wall shelving system, office, kitchen, laundry, college dorm room, kids rooms, closets, shelving, rolling gift wrap centers.

Mudrooms are gaining popularity and a customized kit can maximize efficiency. *Courtesy of Rubbermaid®*

Configurations™ Closet System can grow and change with a child's needs. *Courtesy of Rubbermaid®.*

140

An expandable sliding pants rack is one feature of the *Configurations*™ Closet System for a man's closet.
Courtesy of Rubbermaid®.

Windows

Velux-America, Inc.
www.velux-america.com
800-888-3589
Denmark-based company that produces skylights according to unique Scandinavian technology developed specifically because of dark winter days and desire for maximum daylight.

Tie and belt organizer. *Courtesy of Rubbermaid®.*

Index